REDEMPTION

3 PARISH PASSION PLAYS

BY

GERALD GURKA

M.DIV., M.TH., MA

Published by ScriptWorks Press, 2009
Reprinted and Distributed by WordsonStage.net,2017

Cover Image: Road to Calvary by Simone Martini, The Louvre Museum

Contents

Fallen Angels   Page........4

The Crossmaker   Page....116

The Centurion   Page....158

FALLEN ANGELS

BY

GERALD J. GURKA

JESUS AND THE DEVIL©

CAST of CHARACTERS

JESUS: youth/adult......................................the Son of God
GOD the FATHER...........................Supreme Loving Creator
MARY...Mother of Jesus
JOSEPH...Husband of Mary
ETHAN: ....Childhood friend of Jesus/Crossmaker
JOHANNA... Mother of Ethan
CORNELIUS: ....Assistant Centurion
LONGINIUS: ....Head Centurion & Father of Lucas
LUCAS...........................Young Guard, evil Son of Longinius
PONTIUS PILATE......................Roman Procurator of Judea
CLAUDIA PROCLES...........................Wife of Pontius Pilate
SIMON OF CYRENE............... African farmer, helped Jesus
RUFUS......................................Son of Simon of Cyrene
CAIAPHAS............................. High Priest/Enemy of Jesus
JOHN......................................Beloved Disciple of Jesus
JUDAS.............................Treasurer of Disciples & Traitor
MARY MAGDALENE...........Galilean Woman cured by Jesus
VERONICA...........................Used veil to wipe Jesus' face
VERONICA'S SON.........................Adopted child of Veronica
CONRAD...the 4th Wise Man
TIRA......................................Mother of Dismas & Lucas
GESTAS' MOTHER................. .. Jerusalem drunk & harlot
SAMARITAN WOMAN... .Outcast Woman helped by Jesus
SOFIA...................................... Morally loose Woman
WOMEN of JERUSALEM............. .Vigilantes for Criminals
ARCHANGEL GABRIEL........... .....God's Primary Messenger
ARCHANGEL MICHAEL.................. ..Satan's Adversary
ARCHANGEL RAPHAEL...............................God's Healer
ANGELS........................ Mediators/Messengers of God
LUCIFER.............................Fallen Angel/Prince of Darkness

ANGEL/MRS. SATAN....... .Fallen Angel Spouse of Lucifer
SON of SATAN............ .Eager upstart Prince of Darkness
DAUGHTER of SATAN..... Conniving Princess of Darkness
GUARDS.......................... Assistants to the Centurions
YOUNG CENTURION.............Ruthless apprentice Centurion
BLIND YOUTH...Cured by Jesus
TWO YOUNG CHILDREN.........................Helpers of Jesus
GESTAS.............................Bad Thief crucified with Jesus,
　　　　　　　　　　　　　　　　Stole from Ethan's Shop
DISMAS.............................Good Thief crucified with Jesus
JOHN THE BAPTIST.................Cousin/Forerunner of Jesus
SALOME............................Stepdaughter of Herod Antipas
HEROD......................................Dissolute, mad-man Ruler
HEROD ANTIPAS............Ruler of Galilee & Uncle/Stepfather
　　　　　　　　　　　　　　　　.........of Herodias
ADAM...First Man
EVE..First Woman, Wife of Adam
CAIN..First Son of Adam & Eve
ABEL..Second Son of Adam & Eve
MOSES....................Leader of Israelites appointed by God
KING DAVID....................................King of Israel & Judah
BATHSHEBA......................Beautiful Wife of Uriah the Hittite
URIAH the HITTITE...................Soldier in King David's Army
SAMSON.............................Judge & mighty Ruler of Israel
DELIAH.................................Seductive Philistine Woman
JOSEPH of ARIMATHEA.................Secret Disciple of Jesus
RUTH...Grandmother of Thomas
THOMAS...Grandson of Ruth
ALTAR SERVER.............................Young Church Acolyte
NARRATORS....................Master Storytellers & "Voices" of
　　　　　　　　　　　　　　　　Main Characters

CREW:

CROSS DESIGN   LIGHTING DESIGN
SOUND DESIGN   MUSIC
HAIR & MAKEUP DESIGN   COSTUMES
PROPS   GREETERS & REFRESHMENTS

SETTINGS: note: these can be pre-set around the performance area A Frame Story: Present Day on the morning of a child's First Communion; Eternity: Heaven: before the Creation of Hell & Earth; Old Testament: The Garden of Eden, Mount Sinai, Ancient Kingdom of Israel; New Testament: The Holy Land: Bethlehem, Jordan River & Jerusalem during Passover Week…from Palm Sunday to Easter Sunday

A NOTE from the AUTHOR:
Ideally, this play should be presented in a church, Making use of the main sanctuary/altar area, at back of sanctuary. The main aisle (inside front doors to the altar) Center Aisle leads to the sanctuary
Lighting: One or two follow spot lights with color gels
Optional: Strobe lighting and fog machine to highlight intense scenes. Additional Lighting may be used.

Music: Pre-recorded music. Church Choir & Instrumentalists/or combination. Special Effects: May be pre-recorded or "live" by use of Props. Props needed are listed, with characters, before each Scene. Glitter/colored pieces of paper may be used to "angel flake."
Narrators: One, voice should read the part marked "NARRATOR."
Ideally: a distinct Narrator Voice should be used for each of the following:
        1) VOICE of RUTH

2) VOICE of THOMAS
3) VOICE of JESUS
4) VOICE of GOD the FATHER
5) VOICE of MARY
6) VOICE of MRS. SATAN
7) VOICE of LUCIFER
8) VOICE of SON of SATAN
9) VOICE of DAUGHTER of SATAN
10) VOICE of ETHAN
11) VOICE of JOHANNA
12) VOICE of CORNELIUS
13) VOICE of LONGINIUS
14) VOICE of LUCAS
16) VOICE of CAIAPHAS
17) VOICE of CONRAD
18) VOICE of TIRA
19) VOICE of GESTAS' MOTHER

DIRECTOR'S WELCOMING ADDRESS

(SPOTLIGHT ON. DIRECTOR)

BLACKOUT

INTRODUCTION

(Lights still out. GRANDMOTHER RUTH, holding a sport coat, & GRANDSON THOMAS, wearing dress pants & shirt with an unfinished tie, are in Front of altar. GOD the FATHER, holding a music director's baton; LUCIFER, ARCHANGELS: MICHAEL, carrying Sword, RAFAEL, GABRIEL & ANGELS at Up Center.)

SCENE 1   FIRST COMMUNION MORNING / HEAVENLY CHOIR

NARRATOR: How many of us remember our First Communion Morning? That special, wonderful day...the excitement...our very nervous stomachs...our parents dressing us for Church.

(LIGHTS UP. RUTH helps THOMAS put on sport coat; she begins to adjust tie)

NARRATOR: *(As RUTH adjusts tie.)* Ruth's grandson, Thomas, asked her...

VOICE of THOMAS: "Grandma, Jesus was so good to everybody...why did they kill Him on a cross?"

NARRATOR: But before Ruth could answer, Thomas asked another question...

VOICE of THOMAS: "Grandma, where did evil come from?"

(LIGHTS UP. GOD the FATHER, up center, "taps" his baton into the air. LUCIFER, ARCHANGELS MICHAEL, RAFAEL, GABRIEL and ANGELS begin singing as a choir. GOD the FATHER musically directs them.)

NARRATOR: Ruth then told Thomas...
 (VOICE of RUTH) "When I was in Religion Class...I was taught that, when God created His Angels *(GOD the FATHER joyfully smiling, bows to Audience.)* He made every Angel good. The Angels, Gabriel, *(GABRIEL humbly bows to Audience)* Lucifer, *(LUCIFER smugly bows to Audience.)* Michael *(MICHAEL, flexing his biceps, bows to Audience)*, and Raphael *(RAPHAEL shyly bows to Audience)* were lead singers in the Heavenly Choir. *(LUCIFER arrogantly steps forward and holds his right hand upward as if bearing a torch; his left hand "thumps" upon his chest as if he were giving*

allegiance to himself. GOD the FATHER shakes his head in disapproval. MRS.SATAN) approvingly looks at LUCIFER)

VOICE of RUTH: Lucifer's name means, "Light Bearer." All the other Angels in Heaven thought that Lucifer was the most beautiful and talented Angel of all. But, sadly, Lucifer began to love himself more than he loved God.

(MICHAEL approaches LUCIFER who pushes MICHAEL away.)

VOICE of RUTH: LUCIFER'S pride got in the way. *(MRS. SATAN sneers at MICHAEL)* Lucifer started a fight…a rebellion… in Heaven.

(LUCIFER punches ANGEL in the face, & then beats ANGEL who falls upon the ground. GOD the FATHER, with great anger approaches LUCIFER warning LUCIFER to stop! LUCIFER, snickering at GOD the FATHER, continues to beat & stomp on ANGEL; who attempts to rise, collapses & dies. LUCIFER laughs then spits upon dead ANGEL.)

VOICE of RUTH: God the Father banished Lucifer from His heavenly kingdom.

(GOD the FATHER approaches LUCIFER, orders him to leave. LUCIFER snarls. ANGEL {MRS.SATAN} approaches & begs GOD the FATHER not to banish LUCIFER.)

VOICE of RUTH: Lucifer wanted to be Number One. His pride transformed him into Satan, the accuser…who we also call the "Prince of Darkness." *(LUCIFER orders ANGEL {MRS.SATAN} to stop begging GOD the FATHER & motions: "Join me.")*

VOICE of RUTH: Lucifer was so clever that he even persuaded other Angels to join his revolt.

(LUCIFER smiles at ANGEL {MRS. SATAN} who nods "yes" then "high-5's" LUCIFER.)

VOICE of RUTH: Thomas, it actually reminds me of my younger days...when, while in high school, many of the other girls were attracted to the bad boys.

(THOMAS looks at RUTH & then waves his finger in disapproval)

NARRATOR: Thomas then said...

VOICE of THOMAS: That's right Grandma, just like at my school...when my classmates join gangs who curse and steal.

(RUTH, smiling at THOMAS, nods approvingly)

VOICE of RUTH: Exactly! And Satan was no different. He formed his own gang which came to be known by the title, "Legion."

(LUCIFER approaches ANGELS & motions to each ANGEL to join him. Two ANGELS, SON of SATAN & DAUGHTER of SATAN, join LUCIFER.)

VOICE of RUTH: But, God the Father would not allow such Darkness to take away the Light of Heaven...

(GOD the FATHER commands MICHAEL & ANGELS to expel LUCIFER, & "fallen" ANGELS (MRS. SATAN, SON & DAUGHTER of SATAN}. MICHAEL draws his sword in warning.)

VOICE of RUTH: ...so He had Saint Michael banish Lucifer and his gang from Heaven.

(MICHAEL, GABRIEL, RAFAEL & ANGELS shove LUCIFER & ANGELS {MRS. SATAN, SON & DAUGHTER of SATAN}. They battle. GOD the FATHER stomps His right foot into ground; He then raises & claps His hands...SOUND EFFECTS: (As GOD the FATHER stomps foot). THUNDER & LIGHTENING, SPECIAL EFFECTS: STROBE & FOG. LUCIFER & 'fallen" ANGELS {MRS. SATAN, SON & DAUGHTER of SATAN} fall backward, as if pushed by an invisible bulldozer. They exit)

VOICE of RUTH: And, ever since, Lucifer and his Army have been roaming the Universe...seeking to add more followers...in the hope that...one day...they will become victorious over God.

(RUTH hugs THOMAS; they approach Center Aisle.)

VOICE of RUTH: Lucifer had his first victory when God created the first man and woman...Adam and Eve. (RUTH & THOMAS enter) They lost paradise by giving into Satan's temptations that they would become like God.

BLACKOUT

VOICE of RUTH: *(During BLACKOUT)* After Lucifer's success with the first human beings, Lucifer then decided to tempt every human. It became his intent to ruin every good relationship. Lucifer wanted to make sure that he--not God--would win more souls. Next, he set his sight on Cain and Abel...the sons of Adam and Eve.

(Lights still out. CAIN & ABEL in Front of altar; Tree, bearing Apples, Center. LUCIFER, bearing a Dagger, MRS. SATAN, SON & DAUGHTER of SATAN are by CAIN; ANGEL MICHAEL & ANGELS by ABEL.)

SCENE 2   CAIN AND ABEL

VOICE of RUTH: *(During BLACKOUT)* Lucifer knew well that, in almost every family, brothers and sisters usually compete with each other…for the highest salary, nicest home and car, best school for their children. Lucifer also knew that Cain was extremely jealous of his brother Abel.

(LIGHTS UP. CAIN, with great disgust, looks at ABEL. CAIN then poses as if he were in a weight-lifting contest.)

VOICE of RUTH: Cain despised the fact that Abel was physically stronger than he.

(CAIN approaches ABEL & motions that he wishes to arm wrestle.)

VOICE of RUTH: Cain's jealousy of his brother was so strong that Cain believed Abel's crops were more pleasing to God.

(CAIN & ABEL arm-wrestle. ABEL wins; he hugs CAIN. CAIN, seething, resists & turns his back to ABEL. ABEL, shaking his head, walks off. LUCIFER, gleefully, approaches CAIN.

VOICE of RUTH: Lucifer was very clever. He led Cain to wrongly believe that God loved Abel more…

(LUCIFER displays/flexes his biceps before CAIN. MICHAEL & ANGELS shudder as if they met a ghost. CAIN turns his back toward LUCIFER.)

VOICE of RUTH: …as they say, "the road to hell is paved with good intentions."

(LUCIFER, takes out Dagger, approaches CAIN, and places Dagger into CAIN'S hands.)

VOICE of RUTH: So, Cain wished to win God's love...all for himself.

(ABEL approaches. He looks upward to heaven & raises hands in prayer.)

VOICE of RUTH: Cain, because of his intense jealousy, and envy, allowed darkness to overcome him.

(LUCIFER, smiling, exits, backwards, to left front. CAIN looks upon Dagger in his hands & then raising Dagger high...slowly approaches ABEL.)

VOICE of RUTH: One day, while his brother Abel was praying in the fields...Cain killed his brother Abel.
(CAIN stabs ABEL in the back. As CAIN withdraws Dagger, ABEL turns toward CAIN "asking" why? ABEL embraces CAIN'S shoulders & then falls dead upon ground. CAIN, horrified, drops Dagger. MICHAEL & ANGELS approach ABEL'S dead body & place hands, as if Blessing, over ABEL. LUCIFER & SATANS, laughing, approach CAIN.)

SOUND EFFECTS: THUNDER, LIGHTENING, SPECIAL EFFECTS: STROBE

VOICE of RUTH: *(As CAIN drops Dagger)* Cain's punishment was his guilt...it prevented him from doing what he loved most...the ability to farm. Farming... the very occupation that Cain had used trying to please God.

(CAIN angrily slams his fist into his palm & then enters Center Aisle: CAIN shamefully bows his head downward, raises his hands & begins to tear out his hair. LUCIFER, laughing, approaches CAIN, but stays somewhat at a distance from him. CAIN starts walking down Center Aisle, slamming his fist, in anger, at the Audience.)

VOICE of RUTH: Sin is not always the complete opposite of goodness...

(SATANS join LUCIFER; they gesture "thumbs down" towards CAIN. Then, LUCIFER & SATANS approach Tree with Apples; each takes an Apple from Tree & then hold Apples outward to Audience.)

VOICE of RUTH: More often, than not, sin results whenever we hand over our good intentions to evil.

(LUCIFER enters Center Aisle, winks at Audience and ferociously takes a bite into Apple.)

NARRATOR: And, usually the reason why we hand our good intentions over to evil is because they do not produce the reaction we demand from God.

(LUCIFER, laughing, spits Apple from his mouth & then throws Apple to ground.)
BLACKOUT

VOICE OF RUTH: *(During BLACKOUT)* Despite Cain's sin, God still protected him. God also blessed Adam and Eve with a third son...whom they called "Seth." His name means "anointed." God loves us so much, that...despite our failings...He continues to nurture His Creation. God delights whenever we allow Him to let us grow.

(Lights are still out. GOD the FATHER, holding Ten Commandments Stone Tablets at Center. All ANGELS flank GOD the FATHER. MOSES kneels in Front of altar. LUCIFER & SATANS at left)

SCENE 3   MOSES

NARRATOR: *(During BLACKOUT)* Through the centuries, God choose various individuals to reveal His love for His people. In late 19 B.C, God asked Abraham and his family to move to the land of Canaan. God promised to make Abraham the "father of a multitude of nations." Abraham is called the founder of the Hebrew people. Despite great temptations, Abraham remained dedicated to God. His descendants became greatly blessed. But, sadly, many of them, when the going got rough, also gave into Lucifer's evil.

(LIGHTS UP. MOSES kneels in Front of altar. SPECIAL EFFECTS: FOG)

NARRATOR: Moses, despite the handicap of a severe speech impediment, was a unique mediator between God and His people. *(MOSES, rising, approaches GOD the FATHER) Moses had many visits with God on Mount Sinai...MOSES bows head & kneels before GOD the FATHER, who bids MOSES to rise. GOD the FATHER hands MOSES the Stone Tablets)*

NARRATOR: *(As GOD the FATHER hands MOSES the Tablets)* There, God handed Moses the Ten Commandments. Commandments which God wished His people to follow.

(MOSES begins reading the Stone Tablets. LUCIFER & SATANS approach, glare at Stone Tablets & somewhat retreat. GOD the FATHER, with great authority, points at the writing on Stone Tablets.) SOUND EFFECTS: THUNDER, LIGHTENING SPECIAL EFFECTS: STROBE FOG. LUCIFER & SATANS glare at Stone Tablets & retreat.)

NARRATOR: *(As GOD the FATHER points at the writing on Stone Tablets.)* God also gave Moses further detailed instructions, which Moses recorded. These instructions are referred to as the "Book of the

Covenant." These laws would guide Moses and his people once they settled into the Promised Land. *(GOD the FATHER motions MOSES to leave.)*

BLACKOUT

NARRATOR: *(During BLACKOUT)* Despite God's loving direction, the people were never satisfied. They murmured against God and Moses. They allowed Lucifer and his Legion to revel in planting seeds of disruption in the garden of their minds, hearts and souls. Despite God's continued Blessings, they were never pleased. Lucifer delighted when some of God's people decided to worship other gods...because it was easier...or more fun... than keeping the Ten Commandments. Lucifer incited many to seek pleasure above everything... rather than be moral and upright people...people who could live with their consciences.

SCENE 4   SAMSON AND DELIAH

(Lights still out. SAMSON, carrying Sword, kneeling, & DELILAH, standing, Up Center, ANGELS GABRIEL, MICHAEL & RAPHAEL at left, LUCIFER, holding Scissors, & MRS. SATAN, holding Chains, at right front; TWO GUARDS at Center Aisle Two Pillars are set in Center Aisle/about midway.)

NARRATOR: *(During BLACKOUT)* In trying to be like their neighbors, God's Chosen People forgot who they were. Evil has a way of influencing us to abandon who... and what we love most. *(LIGHTS up DELILAH massages SAMSON'S shoulders and back.)* As a result, God's people often found themselves overpowered by conquering forces...who put them into forced labor.

(SAMSON rises & stretches his arms and muscles—as if a super hero were posing.)

NARRATOR: *(After SAMSON rises)* However, God helped to protect His people by giving them, what we would call today, "Superheroes." Yes, Biblical Superheroes who made a commitment to live a holy lifestyle.

(DELILAH stands behind SAMSON and massages his arms.)

NARRATOR: As described in the Old Testament's Book of Numbers, these warriors made vows--which included various types of abstinence.

(DELILAH, using her fingers, begins to "comb" SAMSON'S hair.)

NARRATOR: Samson was one such warrior. He vowed to never cut his hair…a prayerful gesture of gratitude for the strength God had given him.

(SAMSON goes altar, once there he raises Sword, flexes his arm & chest muscles—looking too self-pleased. ANGEL GABRIEL approaches SAMSON. LUCIFER, holding Scissors high, approaches DELILAH))

NARRATOR: Before Samson was born, an Angel had told Samson's father, Manoah, that His son, Samson, would rescue God's people from the evil of the Philistines.

(LUCIFER takes DELILAH'S right hand & places Scissors into palm.)

NARRATOR: Sadly, Samson's moral strength did not equal his incredible physical strength…

(DELILAH, holds Scissors high, approaches SAMSON from behind. DELILAH, using her left hand, begins to soothe SAMSON'S arm muscles which hold the Sword.)

NARRATOR: ...especially in the relations Samson had with women. Samson's love affair with a woman named Delilah proved to be his undoing...for Delilah was bribed, by the Philistines, to learn the secret of Samson's strength.

(SAMSON, tautly, flexes his muscles. DELILAH holds high a strand of SAMSON'S hair—cutting it off; LUCIFER laughs & ANGEL GABRIEL weeps.)

SPECIAL EFFECTS: STROBE

(DELILAH, holding up the cut strand of hair begins to wickedly laugh. SAMSON, with taut muscles becoming limp, falls to ground upon his knees. DELILAH, laughing, dangles the cut hair in front of SAMSON'S face. Then, DELILAH throws the strand of hair against SAMSON'S chest. TWO GUARDS begin to walk down Center Main Aisle. ANGEL RAPHAEL approaches SAMSON.)

NARRATOR: *(As DELILAH throws strand of hair on SAMSON'S chest)* The Philistines took Samson captive...

(TWO GUARDS use their fingers to poke out SAMSON'S eyes. ANGEL RAPHAEL, standing behind & outstretches hands--as if in "healing" Blessing—over SAMSON, GUARDS & LUCIFER laugh. ANGEL GABRIEL bows head downward. DELILAH throws Scissors to ground.)

NARRATOR: ...they blinded him.

(GUARDS force SAMSON to stand. Then, MRS. SATAN, as if relishing dessert, approaches SAMSON and, using Chain, begins to wrap Chain around SAMSON'S torso. ANGEL MICHAEL approaches SAMSON.)

NARRATOR: They also chained him to a millstone...to grind grain.

(LUCIFER, snickering & using end of Chain, pulls SAMSON into Center Aisle. ANGEL MICHAEL, with arms outstretched, follows SAMSON.)

NARRATOR: During a major festival, the Philistines made a major spectacle of their captive.

(LUCIFER pulls SAMSON down Center Aisle)

NARRATOR: They paraded Samson about the temple. Samson fervently prayed to God for a final victory.

(SAMSON, stopping by Two Pillars placed in aisle, looks upward & then raises arms in a "praying" position—as if begging the heavens. ANGEL MICHAEL stands behind SAMSON & then raises arms upward. SAMSON then lowers his arms, stretching them outward: sideways. LUCIFER, with great horror, looks upon SAMSON'S outstretched arms.)
NARRATOR: Samson recovered his strength.

(SAMSON then lowers his arms & stretches/pushes them out sideways...knocking down Two Pillars. L.UCIFER runs down Center Aisle...exits.)

NARRATOR: SAMSON knocked down two major pillars which collapsed the temple...

SOUND EFFECTS: COLLAPSE of PILLARS

BLACKOUT

NARRATOR: *(After SOUND EFFECTS / During BLACKOUT)*
...killing everyone...including himself. Samson sacrificed himself to protect his people from evil Philistine leaders. This heroic act was a sign that Samson was received back into God's grace. Despite his

faults, Samson, through death, was able to bring about justice. Ultimately, Samson reminds us that we should never allow others to take away our goodness. The story of Samson is a powerful reminder that it is never too late to return to the love and care of God.

(Lights still out. BATH-SHEBA, holding Sun Tan Lotion, is "posing" & URIAH the HITTITE, carrying Sword, & holding Lotion, at Center. KING DAVID, carrying Ring & Sun Tan Lotion, holds Binoculars to his eyes, at Center. LUCIFER, MRS. SATAN, SON of SATAN & DAUGHTER of SATAN YOUNG GUARD, armed with Sword, at right. ANGELS MICHAEL, RAPHAEL & TWO GUARDS at left front.)

SCENE 5   KING DAVID

NARRATOR: *(During BLACKOUT)* However, even the best of God's people--on occasion--regrettably forget about God

(LIGHTS UP: BATH-SHEBA seductively applies Suntan Lotion to her arms, at Top Center)

NARRATOR: Lucifer knows how to use the sin of lust...to his best advantage...as in the case of King David.

(KING DAVID, "salivating" & holding Binoculars focused on BATH-SHEBA, marches down stage, pauses at Front, drops his Binoculars, looks admiringly at BATHSHEBA...KING DAVID watches URIAH the HITTITE applying Sun Tan Lotion to BATH-SHEBA'S back.)

NARRATOR: *(As KING DAVID drops Binoculars)* Like Adam and Eve, we love the forbidden fruit. Like God's Chosen People, we often forget who we are.

(MRS. SATAN & ANGEL RAPHAEL approach BATH-SHEBA. LUCIFER, rubbing his hands together as if creating a flame & ANGEL MICHAEL approach KING DAVID.)

NARRATOR: Jealousy, …wanting what is not rightfully ours…and wanting others not to have it either…invites evil into our life.

(LUCIFER taps KING DAVID upon the shoulder & then points to BATH-SHEBA. LUCIFER proceeds to bow before KING DAVID. Upon rising, LUCIFER makes the gesture: "Go get her!" ANGEL MICHAEL motions "No" to KING DAVID. URIAH the HITTITE hugs BATHSHEBA.)

Voice of URIAH the HITTITE: And, when we do, we often don't realize the great riches we willingly throw away. At these moments, we kid ourselves into thinking we can get away with it…God won't see…nor will anyone else.

(URIAH the HITTITE kisses BATH-SHEBA on her cheek & exits. There: URIAH the HITTITE greets & "high-5's" KING DAVID & then URIAH the HITTITE steps into Center Aisle & exits. MRS. SATAN begins to "massage" BATH-SHEBA'S back. ANGEL RAPHAEL gestures: "No!" to BATH-SHEBA, who, noticing KING DAVID, becomes "enthralled." KING DAVID holds Sun Tan Lotion outward & approaches BATH-SHEBA.)

NARRATOR: David was a Hebrew shepherd boy whom God had blessed with many talents. He was a harpist in the court of King Saul. David rose to fame when he killed the predator giant, Goliath…with only one stone and one pull from his slingshot.

(KING DAVID & BATH-SHEBA embrace. BATH-SHEBA then stares into KING DAVID'S eyes.)

NARRATOR: David's warrior feats won him great admiration...just as King David was now admiring Bath-Sheba...who enjoyed sunning herself atop the palace roof.

(MRS. SATAN & LUCIFER, approvingly, nod   ANGELS MICHAEL & RAPHAEL point fingers in disapproval. MRS. SATANS bids BATH-SHEBA to kneel upon ground. LUCIFER pats KING DAVID upon back & then directs KING DAVID to apply Sun Tan Lotion to BATH-SHEBA'S back; KING DAVID applies Sun Tan Lotion in circular motion. ANGELS MICHAEL & RAPHAEL, saddened, bow their heads.)

NARRATOR: Bath-Sheba was the wife of David's Army Commander, Uriah the Hittite. Uriah was also King David's friend.

(BATH-SHEBA, feeling guilty, stands & motions: "NO MORE!" to KING DAVID. URIAH the HITTITE, brandishing Sword as if in battle, marches down the aisle, as URIAH the HITTITE stares, in great disapproval, at BATH-SHEBA & KING DAVID.)

NARRATOR: .Uriah was instrumental in helping David with his most historic achievement...the capture of Jerusalem from the Philistines...and making Jerusalem the religious Capital of a united Northern State of Israel and Southern State of Judah.

(BATH-SHEBA, whose eyes never leave KING DAVID, exits right. LUCIFER motions to KING DAVID: "How can you let her go...do something!" ANGELS MICHAEL & RAPHAEL intercept LUCIFER & warn: "NO!" to KING DAVID. MRS. SATAN laughs.)

SOUND EFFECT: LAUGHTER

NARRATOR: Satan often tempts us to make ourselves God...to live by our own rules...to the exclusion of the commandments...and, then make ungodly decisions...as did King David.

(KING DAVID, turning to Audience, "finger whistles" SOUND EFFECTS: LOUD WHISTLE. TWO GUARDS, hurriedly, approach & salute KING DAVID.)

NARRATOR: David conspired to have Uriah the Hittite killed. He had Uriah placed in battle...in a position... that would allow no survivors.

(KING DAVID exits. As he exits: URIAH the HITTITE enters Center. YOUNG GUARD, carrying Sword, "scouts" the Audience. LUCIFER approaches YOUNG GUARD & points to approaching URIAH the HITTITE. YOUNG GUARD raises Sword. LUCIFER gestures to YOUNG GUARD: "Slit his throat!")

NARRATOR: David invited evil into his life so that he could marry Uriah's widow, Bath-Sheba.

(URIAH the HITTITE, raising Sword, goes to altar. YOUNG GUARD attacks URIAH. They battle. YOUNG GUARD plunges & twists Sword into URIAH the HITTITE'S abdomen for a slow count of ten; URIAH, in shock, reacts. YOUNG GUARD, while twisting Sword in URIAH'S abdomen, & LUCIFER smile to each other. YOUNG GUARD withdraws Sword. URIAH staggers into Center, takes a few steps, then collapses dead. LUCIFER gestures: "Thumbs up" to YOUNG GUARD & then places his arm around YOUNG GUARD'S shoulders. ANGELS MICHAEL & RAPHAEL, with heads bowed, extend hands, as if in Blessing, over URIAH'S body. MRS. SATAN approaches & laughs into ANGELS' FACES. SOUND EFFECTS: GLEEFUL LAUGHTER. (MRS. SATAN, LUCIFER & YOUNG GUARD exit to left. As SATANS & YOUNG GUARD exit: KING DAVID, enters, & BATHSHEBA, enters from opposite. They meet, they embrace. KING DAVID takes BATH-SHEBA'S hand. then kneels / presents Ring in "proposal." BATH-SHEBA nods: "Yes" to

KING DAVID who proceeds to place Ring on BATH-SHEBA'S finger. BATH-SHEBA guiltily smiles at KING DAVID.)

NARRATOR: God would reprimand David's sinfulness through the words of Nathan the Prophet.

(As BATH-SHEBA guiltily smiles at KING DAVID, BLACKOUT)

NARRATOR: Bath-Sheba gave birth to David's child. The child died within a week. King David's life was a combination of both good and evil. David bitterly repented of the evil he had done. Later, He and Bath-Sheba had a son who survived. Their son would become King Solomon...who became known as the wisest of all rulers. But, Solomon...like his father, David, deceived himself. King Solomon angered God by not taking his faith seriously. Solomon allowed his faith to be like a buffet...where we only pick and choose what we want, without caring what God would want...and Lucifer loves the buffets of human hearts and souls... when they have no appetite for a steady spiritual diet.

(LIGHTS UP. LUCIFER, MRS. SATAN, SON of SATAN & DAUGHTER of SATAN approach altar; there: SATANS "scout" & gestures to Audience: "Come with me/join us!" SATANS, walk/pause & interact with Audience as they exit Center Aisle.)

NARRATOR: Yes, both Solomon and David were deceived by evil...just as Samson was deceived by Delilah...as Cain was deceived by his insecure jealousy, and as Lucifer was deceived by his own vanity...misperceptions abound throughout the remainder of the Old Testament.

NARRATOR: *(As SATANS enter)* Yet, God always remained faithful to His people...even when His people did not remain faithful to Him.

NARRATOR: *(SATANS begin to exit)* God made a Covenant built upon Unconditional Love. God loved His people and wanted them to keep this Covenant. And so, for centuries, God sent Prophets…such as Isaiah, Jeremiah and Ezekiel…to remind His people of His great love and faithfulness.

BLACKOUT

NARRATOR: Eventually, the evilness of God's people would lead to their downfall. Jerusalem and its Temple would be destroyed. And as they fell, Lucifer and his Legions rejoiced. However, God never stopped loving His people…He continued to send Prophets who would guide them back to God's compassion and love. God even promised to send His people a Messiah so that they could restart their life…a restart which was especially needed when their lives fell under Roman rule.

(Lights still out. KING HEROD at Center, LUCIFER, holding Scroll & armed with Sword; MRS. SATAN, SON & DAUGHTER of SATAN at right. MARY, holding INFANT JESUS, & JOSEPH, surrounded by ANGELS GABRIEL, MICHAEL, & RAPHAEL at Center. JOHANNA, holding INFANT ETHAN, at left. YOUNG LONGINIUS, armed with Sword, & YOUNG CORNELIUS, armed with Sword, at Center. VERONICA, holding INFANT, MARY MAGDALENE, holding INFANT, & WOMEN, holding INFANTS, at right.)

SCENE 6   KING HEROD & JESUS' BIRTH & HOLY INNOCENTS

NARRATOR: King Herod was known as "the Great." Even though he was not Jewish, Herod did respect the Jewish faith.

(LIGHTS UP. KING HEROD, in narcissistic style, coming down aisle & jeers at Audience. He walks to Front of altar, turns and bows. LUCIFER approaches & greets KING HEROD in a "fake fraternity-style.)

NARRATOR: *(As KING HEROD reaches altar.)* He rebuilt the Temple in magnificent style. Herod also respected their leaders known as the Pharisees. In addition, Herod built many fine cities throughout the Kingdom.

NARRATOR: *(As LUCIFER approaches KING HEROD)* Yet, Lucifer knew that despite all these wonderful accomplishments King Herod never really won the hearts of the Jewish people, and because Herod was not Jewish…they nicknamed him "the Foreigner." *(LUCIFER presents Sword to KING HEROD.)*

NARRATOR: Lucifer always ready to move in…on people…who feel under-appreciated, knew that Herod was a ripe target.

(LUCIFER slyly smiles as KING HEROD accepts Sword. KING HEROD, delighted, looks upon Sword & then brandishes Sword as if engaged in battle. LUCIFER applauds KING HEROD.)

NARRATOR: *(As KING HEROD swings Sword.).* Herod was ruthless. He would kill anyone he felt was a threat to his power. *(KING HEROD, aiming Sword "in searching style" at Audience, steps to Center. There: KING HEROD thrusts Sword as if to kill. LUCIFER claps in delight.)*

NARRATOR: Herod even had his own sons murdered when he felt they were a threat to his succession.

(KING HEROD, with great anger, uses Sword gesturing: "slit their throats!" LUCIFER, raising hands high, applauds. KING HEROD, becomes still, grimaces & then looks upward to the heavens.)

SOUND EFFECTS: LIGHTENING /THUNDER; LIGHTS, STROBE

NARRATOR: King Herod also knew well the prophecies that God promised a Savior...whose birth would be surrounded by miraculous events.

BLACKOUT

(Lights still out. KING HEROD & LUCIFER walk to Front of altar...then go to (r) of altar.)

NARRATOR: Yes, the Prophet Isaiah predicted that a Savior would be born of a Virgin...in the town of Bethlehem.

(LIGHTS up: MARY, holding INFANT JESUS, JOSEPH & ANGELS at Center. JOHANNA, holding INFANT ETHAN, greets MARY & JOSEPH. As JOHANNA greets MARY & JOSEPH, she presents INFANT ETHAN to MARY. JOHANNA & MARY smile at each other: acknowledging the blessing of their children. KING HEROD, looking threatened & LUCIFER, looking disgusted, stare at each other. LUCIFER shoves KING HEROD into Aisle...there: LUCIFER hands Scroll to KING HEROD...who takes / unrolls Scroll...and then presents Scroll to Audience. VERONICA, MARY MAGDALENE & WOMEN, holding INFANTS, to altar.)

NARRATOR: *(As KING HEROD presents Scroll to Audience.)* Wanting his people to know no other savior than himself, King Herod decreed that a census be taken of the entire kingdom. It was Herod's scheme to find, capture, and even kill the newborn king.

(ANGELS, shivering, raise arms outward/high, as if to form a "brigade shield;" they approach MARY, holding INFANT JESUS, JOSEPH & JOHANNA, holding INFANT ETHAN. KING HEROD, looking as if about to regurgitate, raises his hands up, then slowly claps: YOUNG LONGINIUS & YOUNG CORNELIUS start down aisle & upon reaching KING HEROD, bow. KING HEROD, with great disgust, turns and points to VERONICA, MARY MAGDALENE & WOMEN.)

NARRATOR: *(As KING HEROD points to WOMEN)* When King Herod learned that a Baby King was born; he ordered that every boy in Bethlehem, and its neighborhoods, who was two years old and younger…must be killed.

(ANGELS, with raised arms as if a "brigade shield," walk in front of MARY, holding INFANT JESUS, JOSEPH & JOHANNA, holding INFANT ETHAN. KING HEROD exits; SATANS, applauding, approach YOUNG LONGINIUS & YOUNG CORNELIUS who rise to their feet.)

NARRATOR: Many roads detour us from our original innocence.

(LUCIFER, whistles. then points to VERONICA, MARY MAGDALENE & WOMEN; SATANS gesture: "slit their throats!" YOUNG LONGINIUS & YOUING CORNELIUS, drawing Swords, approach altar.)

NARRATOR: We kill ourselves and our families by giving into the evil of uncontrolled passions, ambitions, jealousies, selfishness, envy…greed.

(LONGINIUS tears INFANT away from MARY MAGDAELNE'S protective arms: throwing INFANT to ground; CORNELIUS stares in disbelief. LONGINIUS orders CORNELIUS to draw Sword & keep WOMEN from escaping. CORNELIUS, shaking, draws & points Sword at WOMEN. LONGINIUS raises Sword high, then slaughters MARY MAGDALENE'S INFANT. ANGELS bow their heads & weep. SATANS applaud. MARY MAGDALENE, beyond grief, collapses upon round. LONGINIUS "rips" INFANT from VERONICA'S arms: throwing INFANT to ground.)

NARRATOR: Perhaps, Mary Magdalene and Veronica lost their children in this blood fest raid…

(LONGINIUS slaughters INFANT. VERONICA, falling upon her knees, removes her Veil & covers slaughtered INFANT. CORNELIUS points Sword at WOMEN, LONGINIUS then slaughters INFANTS in same fashion.)

NARRATOR: *(As LONGINIUS approaches WOMAN)* ...a raid in which Lucifer and his Legions continue to rejoice: the loss, killing of the unborn that no one sees.

(LONGINIUS continues slaughtering INFANTS, feeling sick. WOMEN, falling to the ground, mourn their slaughtered INFANTS. CORNELIUS, in shock, withdraws his Sword. LONGINIUS, approaches altar. CORNELIUS pauses...looks back at LONGINIUS...then runs up center Aisle, flashes the "Loser sign" at CORNELIUS. SATANS snicker & laugh. ANGELS, remaining in place, raise arms higher as if asking God: "Please have mercy!")

NARRATOR: A woman, named Johanna visited the manger that night. She and her infant son, Ethan, would be spared by the same protective Angel wings which guarded Mary, Joseph and their newborn son, Jesus. From that time onward, Johanna and Ethan became close friends with Jesus, Mary and Joseph. Yet, friendships also take their detours. *(LONGINIUS turns away as he is sick. SATANS, clenching their hands into a fist, give a rousing cheer.)*

NARRATOR: Little did Mary, Jesus, Johanna, Ethan, Veronica and Mary Magdalene know that they would meet this young Centurion, once again, on a fateful Friday...some thirty years later.

(LONGINIUS exits. SATANS laugh, and LUCIFER forms his hand into a "Periscope," and "scouts" Audience. SATANS then imitate LUCIFER. SATANS slowly walk down aisle, urging Audience members to join them.)

NARRATOR: Lucifer rejoices at times like these...when loving, innocent families suffer senseless, unexplainable, horrible tragedies.

Lucifer especially loves when people decide to stop living... because of the pain which comes from their loss. Lucifer finds comfort in the moment when people choose to stop loving themselves. Lucifer also revels in the moments when people stop loving those who survive.

(SATANS drop their "Periscopes," rub their hands together in glee & begin to "salivate!")

NARRATOR: Satan enjoys it when anyone feels left behind; those painful, isolated moments when we think our whole world is smashed to pieces by some cosmic jack hammer...which seems to have been aimed directly at our lives.

BLACKOUT

NARRATOR: *(During BLACKOUT)* Yes, during these moments of loss, Satan takes advantage of our pain...setting his sights on us...desiring to win more recruits. The Holy Family of Jesus, Mary and Joseph were not to be immune from Lucifer's attempted gain.

(Lights are still out. MARY sits, her head in her hands. YOUNG JESUS places his hand on MARY'S shoulder. JOHANNA & YOUNG ETHAN are with MARY. LUCIFER, holding a red Handkerchief, MRS. SATAN, holding a Rose, SON of SATAN & DAUGHTER of SATAN at right, ANGEL RAPHAEL kneels before MARY & Jesus, ANGEL MICHAEL is (r) of MARY. ANGEL GABRIEL is (l) of JESUS.)

SCENE 7   JOSEPH'S DEATH

NARRATOR: *(During BLACKOUT)* Mary's husband, Joseph was a carpenter. With great love, Joseph taught Jesus, and his young friend, Ethan...who was spared that night at the manger...the mastery of shaping wood. Later, Ethan, as an adult, would use these carpentry skills for the construction of crosses. The occupation of Crossmaker was a fine paying, full-time position in the Roman Empire. Roman officials loved to hang and crucify their criminals on crosses which would line the entryways to their city. Crosses, with their rotting bodies of convicted criminals, were a blatant advertisement to think twice before committing a crime...to think twice before crossing any Roman official. As an adult, Ethan the Crossmaker would come to revel in the profit that he made from the expense of others' lives.

(LIGHTS UP.   MARY, JOSEPH, YOUNG JESUS, JOHANNA, YOUNG ETHAN, & ANGELS at Center: ANGELS bow to MARY. LUCIFER pretends to cry in handkerchief.)

NARRATOR: Jesus was a better craftsman than his friend, Ethan. Jesus...as an adult...would use his talent not for making crosses, but, for crafting parables and miracles.

(LUCIFER, still "crying" in handkerchief, approaches MARY.)

NARRATOR: Saint Joseph is the patron saint of workingmen.

(LUCIFER bows before JOSEPH'S body. ANGEL RAPHAEL rises & raises wings to protect MARY. JOHANNA, looking alarmed, places her hand on MARY'S shoulder.)

NARRATOR: Lucifer also knows how to be a workingman... working over our hearts and spirits whenever we lose a mother, father, child, loved one or friend.

(LUCIFER, stretching arms outward in sympathetic gesture, places his hands on MARY'S shoulders.)

NARRATOR: During those tragic times, we feel as if we are dropped into an empty desert...with all new temptations. On this day of Joseph's death, Lucifer would not miss the opportunity to test Mary and Jesus. *(LUCIFER, bending downward, whispers into MARY'S ear. ANGEL MICHAEL draws & raises Sword in alarm.)*

NARRATOR: Lucifer whispered into Mary's heart:

VOICE of LUCIFER "Why should you trust God now? Look what He's done to you! He's left you with no job *(LUCIFER points to YOUNG JESUS)* and a young mouth to feed!"

(MRS. SATAN approaches MARY; SON of SATAN, snickering, & DAUGHTER of SATAN, snickering, approach YOUNG JESUS. ANGEL GABRIEL raises arms in a protective stance over YOUNG JESUS.)

NARRATOR: Lucifer's family continued their assault. *(MRS. SATAN stands before MARY.)*

NARRATOR: Mrs. SATAN smirked:

VOICE of MRS. SATAN: A lot good it did you...to always say "yes" to God! *(MRS. SATAN throws her Rose onto JOSEPH'S body.)*

VOICE of MRS. SATAN: Look where it got you...a widow at an early age!

(SON of SATAN & DAUGHTER of SATAN, thump their chests & approach YOUNG JESUS. YOUNG ETHAN also approaches YOUNG JESUS & places his hand on JESUS' shoulder.)

NARRATOR: As YOUNG SATANS, thump their chests, approach YOUNG JESUS, Satan's children snicker at Jesus; they also jeered:

VOICES of SON & DAUGHTER of SATAN: "We still have our father! You Don't! God the Father surely doesn't love you!"

(SON of SATAN & DAUGHTER of SATAN, begin playing an "air fiddle." LUCIFER & MRS. SATAN also "air fiddle." ANGEL MICHAEL, drawing Sword, approaches & demands LUCIFER leave. ANGEL RAPHAEL pushes MRS. SATAN to leave. ANGEL GABRIEL pushes SON of SATAN & DAUGHTER of SATAN to leave. SATANS, laughing / "air fiddling," take few steps backward & then mockingly bow to MARY, YOUNG JESUS & ANGELS.)

NARRATOR: During loss, evil tries to make everything we believe in look wrong. *(SATANS turn to Audience & flash a "self-satisfied" smirk.)*

BLACKOUT

NARRATOR: If we allow...evil will take us on a path that pretends to dull our pain. Certainly, Lucifer, and his Legion, knows how much we often enjoy his first offer. Lucifer is always searching...wanting to add greater misery to his company. Whenever we follow the path that evil so freely offers...especially in times of sorrow...the path, initially, seems easier. However, as we journey, we realize that this path becomes more deadly...to our hearts and to our souls. Yes, Lucifer's initial offer appears seemingly "kind." Yet, once we accept it...our behavior becomes deadly...especially to those we still love. But, good messengers never really die...

(Lights still out. ANGEL GABRIEL at altar; ADULT JESUS, JOHN the BAPTIST, holding large Staff & carrying a Seashell filled with water, at Center. HEROD ANTIPAS, LUCIFER, MRS. SATAN, SON of SATAN, & DAUGHTER of SATAN at right, JUDAS, ANGEL MICHAEL & ANGEL RAPHAEL at left. SPECIAL EFFECTS: FOG)

SCENE 8   JESUS' BAPTISM

NARRATOR: *(During BLACKOUT)* The Angel Gabriel had told Mary that God had chosen her to give birth to His Son. Gabriel had also announced the birth of John the Baptist. *(LIGHTS UP. ANGEL GABRIEL reaches outward to Audience. JOHN the BAPTIST starts down aisle.)*

NARRATOR: The Angel Gabriel also said that John the Baptist would be like the Prophet Elijah…and that John would "turn the hearts of parents to their children."

(ANGEL GABRIEL greets JOHN the BAPTIST who then kneels. ANGEL GABRIEL places hands, as if in Blessing, over JOHN the BAPTIST.)

NARRATOR: Some of the Jewish people did perceive John to be the Prophet Elijah…others wrongly thought John to be the Messiah…who would usher in the final age of history.

(SATANS, looking curious & followed by HEROD ANTIPAS, approach JOHN the BAPTIST…yet, stay at a slight distance.)

NARRATOR: And, as the cousin of Jesus, John the Baptist preached that the only way we could escape God's universal judgment is by repentance…and a cleansing from sin.
(JOHN the BAPTIST rises, turns toward Audience & stretches arms outward…as if to embrace Audience.)

NARRATOR: John also preached that he must prepare the way for the Lord.

(SATANS "tip-toe" around JOHN the BAPTIST. ANGEL GABRIEL raises arms high to form a protective shield over JOHN the BAPTIST. HEROD ANTIPAS, looking more curious, remains in place.)

NARRATOR: Of course, evil is never happy when anyone makes way for the Lord...evil will always be beside us...sometimes even sitting with us in the Church Pew.

(MRS. SATAN approaches & kisses JOHN the BAPTIST on the cheek. LUCIFER looks very proud. SON of SATAN & DAUGHTER of SATAN giggle & place their hands over their lips. JOHN the BAPTIST raises Staff and loudly pounds Staff into the ground.)

SOUND EFFECT: POUNDING of STAFF

NARRATOR: *(After pounding stops)* Evil will always gnaw away at goodness...or any attempt we make at goodness.

(ANGEL MICHAEL & ANGEL RAPHAEL hurriedly "flank" JOHN the BAPTIST, raising their arms over him in protection. JOHN the BAPTIST uses Staff, as if a broom, to "sweep" the SATANS away. SATANS bow in mockery to JOHN the BAPTIST & then take a few steps backward. HEROD ANTIPAS, even more curious, steps closer toward JOHN the BAPTIST; JESUS comes down aisle.)

NARRATOR: *(As HEROD ANTIPAS moves closer & JESUS starts down aisle.)* Yet, as they say, "if you can't shoot the messenger, then go after the message."

(ANGEL GABRIEL, stretching arms in welcome, walks to Center; ANGEL GABRIEL follows JESUS as He goes to altar. There, JESUS embraces JOHN the BAPTIST in greeting.)

NARRATOR: Jesus grew in wisdom and insight. When He was ready to start His Public Ministry, Jesus came to the Jordan River to be baptized by John.

(JESUS, with great pride, looks at JOHN the BAPTIST & then nods "Yes." SATANS, become frenzied, hover—like bats around a steeple—around JESUS & JOHN the BAPTIST; who walk to Center...SATANS continue to hover. HEROD ANTIPAS walks to Right. At Center: JESUS genuflects & bows head. JOHN the BAPTIST, raises Seashell high to the heavens, closes his eyes in prayer, opens his eyes and then tilts Seashell to allow Water to pour over JESUS' head. ANGELS, raise arms & heads upward as if in thanksgiving.)

NARRATOR: As Jesus was baptized, a heavenly voice proclaimed:

VOICE of GOD the FATHER: "This is my own dear Son, with Whom I am well pleased."

(JESUS rises. JOHN the BAPTIST & JESUS embrace. HEROD ANTIPAS steps towards JESUS. SATANS convulse & point their fingers...in "I'll get you fashion" at JESUS & JOHN the BAPTIST. JUDAS, looking as if he were to meet his idol, approaches JESUS.)

NARRATOR: Many, that day, decided to follow Jesus--among them was Judas. He was close by--watching the Baptism of Jesus.

(JUDAS greets JESUS with a "high-five!" LUCIFER, seeing JUDAS, snaps his head to attention)

NARRATOR: Sometimes, like Judas, we desire to become close with God...wanting to present Him with our agenda. *(LUCIFER, smiling, "hovers" nearer JUDAS.)*

NARRATOR: Lucifer loves when our minds and hearts block out what God is truly trying to tell us...the times when our minds and hearts only hear what we, ourselves, have to say.

(JESUS, followed by ANGEL GABRIEL, exits to left as HEROD ANTIPAS takes a few steps closer to JOHN the BAPTIST & then stops.)

NARRATOR: Lucifer also rejoices when, we, like King Herod, are attracted to the message of goodness...but remain cowards to live it through.

BLACKOUT

NARRATOR: *(During BLACKOUT)* Jesus' Baptism marked the beginning of his public ministry. In order to prepare for the most important time of His Ministry...like a disciplined athlete...Jesus went to train in the Desert. There, He fasted for forty days and forty nights...a reminder of the forty years Moses and His people traveled in the desert. Lucifer becomes very unhappy whenever we desire to shape our minds, bodies, hearts and souls. Yes, Lucifer will make every effort to undo any good we attempt to do. While training in the desert, Lucifer tempted Jesus...just as he did with Adam and Eve...who had it all, but wanted more. Lucifer will do no less with us. His greatest temptations usually present us with the scenario that...in order to be happy in life... we should be getting more...more than the limits we currently have. After all, shouldn't we have everything we want...all the forbidden fruits that are just a mouse-click away?

(Lights are still out. JESUS, holding a Scroll, is between YOUNG CHILDREN &. ANGELS. MARY, MARY MAGDALENE, & JOHN the APOSTLE, JUDAS, WOMEN of JERUSALEM at left. LUCIFER, carrying Money, MRS. SATAN, SON of SATAN, DAUGHTER of SATAN & CAIAPHAS at right front. LONGINIUS, CORNELIUS, LUCAS & HEROD ANTIPAS at Center)

SCENE 9   TEMPLE

NARRATOR: *(During BLACKOUT)* Jesus' journey into the desert gave Him greater self-knowledge. The desert times in our lives do the same...if only we desire to learn from the pain.

(LIGHTS UP. JESUS unrolls Scroll & raises His hand in proclamation; HEROD ANTIPAS, starts coming down aisle. "investigating" the Audience while walking down aisle.)

NARRATOR: *(As JESUS unrolls Scroll)* It was Jesus' turn to lector in the Temple. Many, in the congregation, had witnessed Jesus' Ministry...and the work of His Disciples.

(CAIAPHAS, yawning & becoming bored, gazes at Audience.)

NARRATOR: Many in the congregation had heard Jesus' Sermon on the Mount as well as His Parables. They also had either seen...or heard about Jesus' many miracles: raising Lazarus from the Dead, curing the Centurion's child, and feeding thousands with food that was only enough to feed a few people.

(WOMEN of JERUSALEM approach JESUS & kneel at His feet. As HEROD ANTIPAS reaches Front of altar, He turns to the audience and makes a "gloating gesture," & then rubs his hands together as if plotting a new scheme.)

NARRATOR: King Herod's son, Herod Antipas, looked and dressed exactly like his father, Herod the Great. But, Herod Antipas' methods were far more sinister than that of his father.

(HEROD ANTIPAS, squinting eyes at Audience, & then approaches JESUS. MARY, MARY MAGDALENE & JOHN the APOSTLE, closely watching HEROD ANTIPAS, take a few steps forward.)

NARRATOR: Yet, Herod Antipas was very curious about Jesus' ministry. He also was jealous of Jesus' popularity.

(HEROD ANTIPAS halts & begins tapping his finger upon his lips. LUCIFER, gesturing" "thumbs down," approaches HEROD ANTIPAS.)

NARRATOR: (As LUCIFER makes "thumbs-down" gesture.) Do we try to destroy the reputation of others because of our jealousy?

(MRS. SATAN, raising fist, approaches LONGINIUS; SON of SATAN, raising fist, approaches CORNELIUS; DAUGHTER of SATAN, raising fist, approaches LUCAS: SATANS encourage LONGINIUS, CORNELIUS & LUCAS to raise fists in protest against JESUS. CAIAPHAS then raises his fist in protest.)

NARRATOR: Herod Antipas feared that Jesus' great influence as well as the influence of John the Baptist…would provoke the people to revolt. (HEROD ANTIPAS approaches LONGINIUS & gestures: "Throw JESUS out!" LONGINIUS directs CORNELIUS & LUCAS to seize JESUS. SATANS, gleefully, jump up & down. ANGELS reach outward to JESUS. CORNELIUS, looking hesitant, & LUCAS, looking very eager, seize JESUS & bend him downward…head-first…as if a log to ram down a castle door. ANGELS shudder. MARY hurries to JESUS; LUCAS gestures to MARY: "STOP!" LUCAS spits upon MARY. ANGELS shudder. CORNELIUS angrily stares at LUCAS. HEROD ANTIPAS snickers. JUDAS, very upset, follows JESUS. CAIAPHAS approaches HEROD ANTIPAS.

NARRATOR: So, Herod began to plot with the Pharisees for a means to destroy Jesus…even though Herod had a strong desire to learn more about being a follower of Jesus. *(HEROD ANTIPAS motions to LONGINIUS that: "JESUS be removed!")*

NARRATOR: Are we like Herod? Do we not listen to what our hearts...our consciences really long for?

(LONGINIUS directs CORNELIUS & LUCAS to shove JESUS, head first, into Center Aisle)

NARRATOR: Or do we let everything else get in the way?

(CORNELIUS, looking more distressed, & LUCAS, wild with abandon, throw JESUS into Center Aisle; JESUS falls. SATANS raise hands making the "Victory" symbol. MARY, stretching hands outward, runs after JESUS. JOHN the APOSTLE & MARY MAGDALENE run after MARY & try to hold her back. ANGELS raise arms, as protection over her. JUDAS stares, in disbelief, at JESUS lying on ground. WOMEN of JERUSALEM, crying, bury their heads into their hands. MRS. SATAN, laughing, gestures the "Loser sign" to MARY. HEROD ANTIPAS, looking self-satisfied, moves Center & "locks" his hands upon his biceps in regal stance. LONGINIUS, like a bodyguard, follows HEROD ANTIPAS. LUCIFER taps JUDAS upon shoulder in a methodical, menacing manner—like rain drops wearing away upon a stone.)

NARRATOR: Judas started to become disappointed in Jesus...He could not understand why Jesus did not try to exert a greater influence over the political authorities. Judas became increasingly disillusioned in Jesus as he realized that Jesus' prime interest was not in political...but spiritual matters.

(LUCIFER places his fingers under JUDAS' chin as if to say: "Judas, why so serious?" LUCIFER then wraps his arms around JUDAS' shoulders as if "best buddies.")

NARRATOR: In our times of greatest disillusionment, Satan is always ready to make a very attractive deal with us.

(LUCIFER dangles Money before JUDAS' eyes. JUDAS attempts to grab Money but LUCIFER, laughing, prevents JUDAS from taking Money; LUCIFER, waves finger, as if to say: "Not yet, Judas!")

NARRATOR: And, Judas, the official treasurer for the Twelve Disciples, was always ready to make a deal...especially when the deal would make him a handsome profit.

BLACKOUT

NARRATOR: *(During BLACKOUT)* Herod Antipas, like his father, was beguiled by power. But beautiful women bewitched Herod even more. Breaking Jewish religious law, Herod married his half-brother's wife...whose name was Herodias. Herodias hated the fact that John the Baptist denounced her marriage to Herod. Herodias' influence was responsible for Herod's decision to have John the Baptist thrown into prison.

(Lights are still out. HEROD ANTIPAS, holding empty goblet, is between LONGINIUS, carrying a blindfold, CORNELIUS; LUCIFER, holding Wine Flask, at altar. MRS. SATAN, holding Sword, at left. JOHN the BAPTIST, hands tied, LUCAS & SALOME, with Finger Cymbals, at Center Aisle. ANGELS MICHAEL & RAPHAEL at left)

SCENE 10   SALOME

NARRATOR: *(During BLACKOUT)* Herodias had a daughter by her first marriage...her name was Salome.

*(LIGHTS UP. HEROD ANTIPAS, LONGINIUS & CORNELIUS at Center;
LUCIFER pours HEROD a drink.)*

NARRATOR: Satan knows well that drinking more than we should
often leads to actions we never would do when we are sober.

*(SALOME, clicking Finger Cymbals, dances down aisle, in a seductive
manner, until reaching altar. HEROD ANTIPAS consumes wine & LUCIFER
gladly refills)*

NARRATOR: Herod was entranced by Salome's beauty.

*(SALOME genuflects before HEROD ANTIPAS who grins as if he were a pig
in butter.)*

NARRATOR: He foolishly promised Salome anything she wanted.

*(SALOME rises, kisses HEROD ANTIPAS on the cheek & then whispers into
his ear. HEROD'S smile turns into a frown. LUCIFER flashes a snide smile)*

NARRATOR: Prompted by her mother, Salome asked for the head of
John the Baptist on a plate.

*(LUCAS forces JOHN the BAPTIST Center, then throws JOHN the BAPTIST
down in front of HEROD ANTIPAS. LUCAS steps on JOHN the BAPTIST'S
back. LUCIFER motions: "YES!" ANGELS MICHAEL & RAPHAEL stand at
JOHN the BAPTIST'S left and right, they pray over him.)*

NARRATOR: Like Herod, we sometimes make promises that are
beyond reason. And also like Herod, sometimes we do not have the
courage to admit that we made a mistake.

(MRS. SATAN hands LUCIFER a Sword. LUCIFER offers Sword to CORNELIUS who angrily takes Sword & throws it to ground. LUCIFER slaps CORNELIUS across the face. LUCAS retrieves the Sword.)

NARRATOR: We can silence physical, exterior voices; but we can never silence the voices of our conscience...even when we try to drown them.

(SALOME sadistically laughs & exits. HEROD ANTIPAS orders LONGINIUS to raise JOHN the BAPTIST up on his feet & blindfold him. LUCIFER hands the Wine Flask to HEROD who drinks it dry. LONGINIUS turns JOHN the BAPTIST to face Audience. LUCAS, still holding Sword, forces JOHN the BAPTIST to kneel & bends JOHN'S head over in preparation for beheading. CORNELIUS, with sadness, observes LONGINIUS & LUCAS. LONGINIUS grabs Sword from LUCAS who spits in LONGINUS' face. LONGINIUS, using both hands, raises Sword high over JOHN the BAPTIST. HEROD ANTIPAS turns his face away. ANGELS sadly bow. LONGINIUS lowers the Sword...and as Sword is about to strike JOHN the BAPTIST'S neck....)

BLACKOUT

SOUND EFFECTS: GROAN SCREAM, THUD

NARRATOR: (During BLACKOUT) Salome's name is never mentioned in the Bible. John the Baptist's influence did not end with his death. Many of the Baptist's followers became disciples of Jesus...and Jesus' influence and popularity continued to grow. Jesus' disciples would come to learn of His Messiahship. They would hear Jesus predict His Passion...and Jesus made it very clear that the Messiah would not be a victorious figure of Jewish political expectations...but one who would suffer, be killed...but, also rise from the dead.

(Lights still out. JESUS, MARY, JOHN the APOSTLE & MARY MAGDALENE at Center; ANGELS at left, SATANS, holding Palms, CAIAPHAS, carrying 40 pieces of silver in Pouch, & JUDAS at right front YOUNG BLIND CHILD, with a cloth around eyes & head, at Center. Remaining CAST, holding Palms, at (r) & (l) of altar.)

SCENE 11   PALM SUNDAY

NARRATOR: (During BLACKOUT) Jesus never preached politics. Yet, on the Sunday before Passover, an outburst of political fervor greeted Jesus when He entered Jerusalem.

(LIGHTS UP. JESUS, MARY, JOHN the APOSTLE, MARY MAGDALENE at Center: JESUS & MARY, followed by JOHN the APOSTLE & MARY MAGDALENE, approach altar. Remaining CAST, waving Palms high, greet JESUS as if He were a winning candidate. SATANS & JUDAS, curiously watching JESUS, go to Center.)

NARRATOR: Evil was also fully in fervor that Palm Sunday.

(JESUS & MARY step Center, as they do: CAST waves Palms and "dances" around JESUS. YOUNG BLIND CHILD starts down aisle: CAIAPHAS, angrily staring at YOUNG BLIND CHILD, approaches SATANS. As YOUNG BLIND CHILD approaches JESUS his hands reach out to "touch.")

NARRATOR: A Young Blind Child was present. He wished to "see" what Jesus was like.

(JESUS, stooping down, takes YOUNG BLIND CHILD'S hands & places them upon His face.)

NARRATOR: This child could see by his sense of touch.

(JESUS removes YOUNG BLIND CHILD'S bandages & touches his eyes; they embrace. CAST, energetically, waves Palms in circular formation)

NARRATOR: For some reason, as we age, we do not allow ourselves to freely ask for Jesus' help. Our Lord urges us not to lose the lovely simplicity of a little child. Maybe...we are really afraid that a miracle may actually happen...a miracle that will call for a change in us.
(MARY, with a mother's pride, smiles at JESUS & together they start down aisle. CAST, waving Palms/dancing/twirling, follow/circle JESUS. ANGELS follow CAST down aisle & continually bow toward JESUS. LUCIFER gives a Palm to CAIAPHAS, who looks at Palm with disgust, throws Palm to ground & then stomps on Palm. MRS. SATAN laughs & hands Palm to JUDAS...who looks at Palm & then tosses Palm over his shoulder. As JUDAS tosses Palm over shoulder: SON of SATAN
& DAUGHTER of SATAN, approach & bow/wave Palms before JUDAS.)

NARRATOR: Nor do we like when others get the attention we thought we deserve. (SATANS & CAIAPHAS wickedly smile at JUDAS) ...as did Judas, that day.

(CAIAPHAS presents Money Pouch to JUDAS, then dangles it before JUDAS' eyes JUDAS holds out both hands in a "gimme" fashion. CAIAPHAS takes one Coin & drops it...LUCIFER, laughing, intercepts Coin before it reaches JUDAS' hands. CAIAPHAS repeats with second Coin which is intercepted by MRS. SATAN. JUDAS attempts to grab Money Pouch from CAIAPHAS who motions: "Let's not be greedy." SATANS "belly laugh.")

NARRATOR: Satan revels when our jealousy of family and friends drives us to emotionally, as well as verbally, sell them out.

(JUDAS tears Money Pouch away from CAIAPHAS' hands. CAIPHAS pats JUDAS on head as if he were a puppy.)

NARRATOR: We sell them out in so many clever ways. Yes, Envy, Jealousy and Greed make deadly friends.

(CAIAPHAS, placing his arm around JUDAS, as if they were winning team mates, walks with him down Center Aisle; SATANS, flashing the "Loser sign," follow them.)

BLACKOUT   MUSICAL INTERLUDE

(Lights still out.   JESUS holding Water Pitcher & Towel across his shoulder, JUDAS, with bare foot, & PETER, holding Wash Bowl, in Front of altar. MARY, MARY MAGDALENE, JOHN the APOSTLE, VERONICA, JOHANNA, ADULT ETHAN, YOUNG CHILDREN are at altar; ANGELS at Center. LUCIFER, holding a Pitchfork, & SATANS at right, Candles, lighted, Cup & Dish, with Bread, are placed upon altar.)

<u>SCENE 12</u>   THE LAST SUPPER

NARRATOR: *(During BLACKOUT)* We celebrate special times with those we love. Families and friends gather for birthdays, anniversaries, graduations, thanksgiving… holidays…with a sumptuous meal. Jesus did the same with His Family…with His Disciples. On a Thursday Night, they celebrated the Passover Meal. This Meal would become known as the Last Supper…as well as the First Mass. It was a wonderful First Communion evening. That Thursday is forever called "Holy."

(LIGHTS UP. JESUS washes JUDAS' feet. PETER & JOHN the APOSTLE suspiciously look upon JUDAS.)

NARRATOR: The meal becomes special, not for what is served, but for who shares it. Being present…together…is more important than the meal itself. *(JESUS, using Towel, wipes JUDAS' foot. PETER puts Wash Bowl down.)*

NARRATOR: These celebrations, with the passing of our loved ones, become memories as well as present realities. In effect, our family tables, our homes, become sacred places.

(JESUS places his arm around JUDAS & stares into JUDAS' eyes. JUDAS looks away. Together, JESUS & JUDAS walk to altar.)

NARRATOR: *(JESUS takes center place at altar)* Family Tables…Altars…Church Tables. Here, love becomes the main ingredient in celebrating the meal. *(JESUS takes Bread & raises for all to see.)*
NARRATOR: Jesus took the bread—said the Blessing, broke it, and gave it to His Disciples, saying:

VOICE of JESUS: "Take it. This is My Body."

(ANGELS bow then raise their hands toward JESUS. SATANS grip their stomachs as if they contacted food poisoning.)

NARRATOR: Then Jesus took the cup and gave thanks.

(JESUS, turning to MARY, presents the Cup; MARY touches the Cup. JESUS then raises the Cup for all to see.)

NARRATOR: He said to His apostles:

 VOICE of JESUS: "This is the blood of the New Covenant that will be shed for many…Do this in Memory of Me."

(ANGELS bow & raise hands toward JESUS. SATANS experience intense abdominal pain. As JESUS lowers the cup, JUDAS looks bored. LUCIFER tip-toes to JUDAS &, using Pitchfork, pokes JUDAS. ANGELS shudder. JUDAS stares at JESUS & takes a few steps away. LUCIFER, smiling, retreats to

right front. MARY approaches JUDAS as if asking: "Is something wrong?" MARY hugs JUDAS, who completely turns his head away from MARY. JUDAS goes to Front of altar, pauses & bows head downward. JOHN the APOSTLE stuffs his mouth with Bread.)

NARRATOR: Satan delights when at these special meals, family resentments, discontentment, unresolved issues raise their ugly heads.

(MARY, followed by JESUS, motions to JUDAS: "It will be okay." JESUS, placing his hand under JUDAS' chin, forces JUDAS to look at Him. JUDAS shoves JESUS away. JOHN the APOSTLE, very upset, approaches JUDAS. ANGELS, raising hands, approach, from behind, JESUS & MARY)

NARRATOR: Judas was disappointed in Jesus. He thought that Jesus would be a political Messiah...rather than a purely spiritual one: similar to the times when parents and children become disappointed in each other.

(JOHN the APOSTLE pushes JUDAS to leave. JUDAS pauses & looks back at JESUS...who stretches his arms outward toward JUDAS...as if to say: "Judas, please come back! You don't have to do this!")

NARRATOR: Adult children often see their older folks as financial messiahs...who have to bail them out of any financial mess. And, sadly, parents sometimes view their children as the saviors of what they were unable to accomplish, with their own sports, homes, or selves.

(LUCIFER, using Pitchfork pokes JUDAS to leave. MRS. SATAN kisses JUDAS on the forehead, then pushing him away. JUDAS, looks back at JESUS. JOHN the APOSTLE motions JUDAS to leave)

NARRATOR: Often, because of misguided expectations, family members wrongly write each other off. Unwilling to see the beauty their loved ones possess, they choose to only see beauty in whatever their expectations dictate.

(SON of SATAN & DAUGHTER of SATAN shove JUDAS down Aisle. JUDAS, looking frightened & confused, walks down the Aisle, interacting with Audience, asking: "Am I doing the right thing? Please tell me I am." LUCIFER raises Pitchfork high. SATANS stomp feet & laugh wildly. LUCIFER pounds Pitchfork into ground.) SOUND EFFECT: PITCHFORK pounding in to ground)

BLACKOUT

NARRATOR: *(During BLACKOUT)* Satan loves to work in the Garden of our hearts and souls. Satan especially loves the moments when we allow him to plant seeds of hate inside us...in effect, pruning off the rose buds instead of the thorns. Jesus loved the Garden. He especially loved to pray in the olive grove at Gethsemane. There, Jesus regularly taught His family of disciples how to pray.

(Lights still out. JESUS & JOHN the APOSTLE at Center. SATANS, holding Packets of seeds, above, ANGELS at left., CAIAPHAS at right. JUDAS, LONGINIUS, holding Spear, CORNELIUS, holding Sword, LUCAS, holding Club, & GUARDS, with Weapons)

SCENE 13   GARDEN   SPECIAL EFFECTS: FOG

NARRATOR: *(During BLACKOUT)* As members of God's Family, what seeds do we plant in the gardens of our lives?

(LIGHTS UP: SATANS, scattering Seeds from their packets onto ground; stomp on the Seeds & rub their hands together in glee. SATANS exit, "tip-toeing," down Aisle)

NARRATOR: Do we plant seeds of love, trust, and forgiveness? Or do we plant seeds of hate and betrayal?

(JESUS & JOHN the APOSTLE encounter the SATANS. LUCIFER, laughing viciously, points finger as if saying: "Just you wait!" at JOHN the APOSTLE; who resists. LUCIFER, in mockery, then presses his finger into JOHN the APOSTLE'S nose.)

NARRATOR: Many times, when we pray, we encounter unexpected interruptions.

(JESUS raises his hand against SATAN, as if saying: "Be gone! You have no power here!" JESUS & JOHN walk to the altar. There, Jesus takes JOHN'S hands & folds them into a "prayerful stance;" ANGELS raise their hands in praise. SATANS, fold hands in a "mock" prayer stance. JOHN, falling upon knees, prayerfully raises his hands upward. JESUS, with great satisfaction, looks upon JOHN.)

NARRATOR: This was Jesus' favorite spot to pray to God His Father.

(JESUS goes to Center. ANGELS gather to JESUS' left and right)

NARRATOR: Tonight, Jesus especially prayed for strength to combat the evil He knew was present.

(JESUS profoundly bows his head. ANGEL RAPHAEL places his head against JESUS' right shoulder. JESUS stretches his hands up to the heavens. JOHN, yawning, rises, looks towards JESUS, then stretches, yawns & falls asleep upon the ground. CAIAPHAS, on tip-toes, approaches JOHN who remains asleep. CAIAPHAS, delighted, rubs hands together in sinister fashion. LUCIFER greets CAIAPHAS with a "high-5". CAIAPHAS bows to LUCIFER & then "slithers" away.)

NARRATOR: Jesus asked His Father for courage and understanding…so should we whenever we face issues and events that we have no control over.

(As CAIAPHAS moves, LUCIFER whistles. JUDAS, followed by LONGINIUS, CORNELIUS, LUCAS & GUARDS, starts down aisle. As JUDAS approaches altar, JOHN awakes/ rises & stares at JUDAS. LUCIFER signals LUCAS to beat JOHN. JOHN runs away to left. As he runs, LUCAS steps on JOHN'S Tunic which rips off JOHN'S body MRS. SATAN, laughing, pretends to cover her eyes. JUDAS pauses & watches JOHN who exits. LUCAS shoves JUDAS closer to JESUS, who remains in prayer. ANGEL MICHAEL, raising Sword, intercepts JUDAS…but, LONGINIUS & LUCAS continue to push JUDAS. CORNELIUS, looking very hesitant, closely observes LONGINIUS & LUCAS. JUDAS…now directly behind JESUS, raises hand & taps JESUS on the back. JESUS, turns and stares at JUDAS.)

VOICE of JESUS: "Judas, do what you have come for." *(MRS. SATAN eerily whispers into JUDAS' ear.)*

NARRATOR: (VOICE of MRS. SATAN as MRS. SATAN whispers into JUDAS' ear) "Just do it!"
 (JUDAS betrays JESUS with a "kiss." ANGELS weep. JUDAS exits: running. LONGINIUS commands CORNELIUS to push JESUS to ground. LUCAS clubs JESUS across the back. GUARDS beat & spit at JESUS. CAIAPHAS, laughing, gleefully rubs his hands together. SATANS raise fists high in form of "V.")

BLACKOUT

NARRATOR: Satan proclaims a victory whenever family members rejoice in the misfortune of others…especially when those who should love us betray us. That night, Jesus' Mother, knew something was very wrong. Loving parents often sense when something horrible is happening to their children. *(Lights still out. MARY in Center, JOHN the APOSTLE, CLAUDIA, with a white linen Towel tied about her belt,*

CORNELIUS, carrying a Flask, JESUS, with hands Rope-tied, LUCAS, carrying a Club & Flask, TWO GUARDS, carrying Flasks, & ADULT ETHAN at Center; PONTIUS PILATE, LONGINIUS, carrying a Flask, CAIAPHAS, JUDAS, SATANS, holding Staffs, at right JOHANNA, VERONICA, MARY MAGDALENE, WOMEN of JERUSALEM, ANGELS at left front. REMAINING CAST at left front & right front.)

PROPS: Crown of Thorns, Red Cloak, Reed, Baby wrapped in swaddling clothes, 4 Whips, 4 Jugs of "spirits."

<u>SCENE 14</u>   NIGHT

NARRATOR: *(During BLACKOUT)* That night, John the Apostle came running to Mary.

(LIGHTS UP. JOHN runs to MARY at Center, greets MARY with a sympathetic embrace.)

NARRATOR: John told her about Jesus and the plans he overheard…that Jesus was to be taken before Pontius Pilate for a Trial. Mary, like every parent, could not understand why such a senseless tragedy would befall her child. *(CLAUDIA, escorted by CORNELIUS, starts down aisle, studies MARY'S face)*

NARRATOR: Claudia Procles was the wife of Pontius Pilate. She dreamt about Jesus the night before. Claudia knew of Jesus' inexhaustible love for people. Claudia's heart went out to Mary. *(MARY, gratefully nods to CLAUDIA, stares at CORNELIUS, who becomes uncomfortable with MARY'S staring.)*

NARATOR: Mary recognized this Centurion. Mary remembered that, several weeks ago, Jesus brought this Centurion's child back to life. *(JOHN bids MARY to leave; they exit. CLAUDIA reaches out to MARY.)*

CORNELIUS looks down upon ground. PONTIUS PILATE, flanked by LONGINIUS, approaches CLAUDIA...who disapprovingly, shakes her head at PONTIUS PILATE. CAIAPHAS, waving an accusatory finger, approaches PONTIUS PILATE. CAIAPHAS gestures: "Let's get on with it!" to PILATE. LONGINIUS signals CORNELIUS to escort CLAUDIA to Center...LONGINIUS then accompanies PONTIUS PILATE, to Center. CAIAPHAS goes to altar, there; he turns & snickers at Audience before he exits)

SCENE 15   TRIAL

NARRATOR: *(As PONTIUS PILATE & CLAUDIA go to Center)* Pontius Pilate was a man of extreme pride and meanness. He was a self-absorbed ruler and husband. Pilate was also excessively superstitious. He and Claudia lived in the same dwelling which once housed King Herod...the mad ruler who was responsible for the murder of the Holy Innocents, at the time of Jesus' Birth.

(LUCAS, using Rope, pulls JESUS, followed by TWO GUARDS, down aisle. TWO GURADS laugh at, spit & kick JESUS. LUCAS throws JESUS down in Front of altar. GUARDS laugh. CORNELIUS sympathetically looks upon JESUS. CLAUDIA, turning to PONTIUS PILATE, raises arms as if to say: "Please don't do this!")

NARRATOR: Claudia told her husband about a dream she had the night before. She urged Pilate not to condemn an innocent man. Claudia reminded Pilate of how Jesus fed the poor. But, like most husbands, Pilate would not listen to his wife.

(LONGINIUS directs LUCAS & TWO GUARDS to bring JESUS before PILATE. They push JESUS to PONTIUS PILATE. As JESUS reaches PONTIUS PILATE, TWO GUARDS trip JESUS, hand He collapses to ground. LUCAS & GUARDS spit upon JESUS. CORNELIUS, with sympathy & sadness, looks at JESUS. LONGINIUS, raising his arm, commands LUCAS &

GUARDS to "STOP!" LONGINIUS raises JESUS to stand. CLAUDIA slaps PONTIUS PILATE across the face. SATANS, stomp their Staffs on the floor, and ANGELS, with outstretched arms go to JESUS.)

SCENE 16   SCOURGING & CROWNING

NARRATOR: Often, we refuse to hear the truth. We refuse to be responsible for our actions. *(PILATE regains composure.)* And, when we refuse to be responsible...we create further evil *(PILATE gestures for JESUS to be removed)* if only, to our conscience. Not wanting to be responsible, Pontius Pilate had Jesus scourged.

(LUCAS & TWO GUARDS shove JESUS. SATANS "mockingly" bow to JESUS & retreat. ANGELS approach JESUS. LUCAS, strikes JESUS across the back. JESUS collapses to His knees. MARY, followed by JOHN & MARY MAGDALENE, runs to JESUS. LONGINIUS prevents MARY from meeting JESUS. CORNELIUS, sadly, looks upon MARY. LONGINIUS turns his face away from MARY. LONGINIUS turns to JESUS, raises Flask as if to propose a toast: CORNELIUS, hesitantly raises Flask, LUCAS & TWO GUARDS readily raise Flasks.)

NARRATOR: The guards started their Celebration of Passover, early.

(LONGINIUS & GUARDS "swig" from Flasks, wipe dry their mouths, then raise Flasks again.)

NARRATOR: The Centurions and guards again raised their flasks to toasts the occasion.

(LONGINIUS & GUARDS guzzle "dry" their Flasks, looking for more, they hold Flasks high, sticking their tongues out, hoping to capture any final drops.)

NARRATOR: As the Centurions and guards arrogantly mocked the traditional Passover toast; Mrs. Satan decided to mock the maternal love that Mary had for her son.

(MRS. SATAN, carrying BABY wrapped in swaddling clothes, approaches MARY... rocking the BABY as if singing a lullaby. As if making a "sacrificial offering," she then presents BABY to MARY & then, laughing loudly, snatches BABY back. SAINT MICHAEL, holding Sword out, forces MRS. SATAN to leave; ANGELS "angel flake" MRS. SATAN who bounces backward as if an invisible force-field shoved her. MRS. SATAN, with a malevolent snicker points her finger at ANGELS as she "slithers"/exits right.)

VOICE of MRS. SATAN: "What kind of mother are you...that you can't even protect your son? Ha! Ha! Ha! Ha! Ha!"

(As MRS. SATAN exits, LUCIFER, approaches LONGINIUS & CORNELIUS; SON of SATAN, carrying two Jugs of "spirits," TWO GUARDS; & DAUGHTER OF SATAN, each carrying a Jug of "spirits," approach LUCAS. SATANS dangle Jugs before CENTURIONS & GUARDS who reach for Jugs. CENTURIONS & GUARDS then take a hearty drink from Jugs.)

NARRATOR: Roman guards often drank hard...so as not to feel the pain of their consciences. They became numb to the pain they inflicted. *(CENTURIONS & GUARDS toss Jugs away.)*

NARRATOR: PONTIUS PILATE was hoping that the crowds would become numb to their cry for Jesus' Crucifixion....so he ordered Jesus to be scourged.

(MARY collapses to ground. JOHN & MARY MAGDALENE console her. CAIAPHAS, gleefully jumping up & down, stays at a distance. DAUGHTER of SATAN, smiling, distributes Whips to CORNELIUS, LUCAS & TWO GUARDS. DAUGHTER of SATAN then goes to watch scourging. LUCAS slaps JESUS across the face & then pushes JESUS. MARY, with

outstretched arms, runs toward JESUS. ANGELS bow toward MARY. LUCAS prevents MARY from reaching JESUS. JOHN the APOSTLE & MARY MAGADALENE run to shield MARY from LUCAS. LONGINIUS raises his right hand to direct TWO GUARDS to stand before JESUS. TWO GUARDS swing their Whips into air. LONGINIUS turns JESUS around: JESUS' back faces Audience. LONGINIUS & TWO GUARDS swing Whips in circular motion & proceed to strike JESUS. MARY faints: JOHN the APOSTLE & MARY MAGDALENE catch MARY.)

NARRATOR: Jesus received forty lashes, tearing His flesh
.

SOUND EFFECTS: WHIPPING   PAINFUL GROANS
SPECIAL LIGHTING: STROBE

(As JESUS is scourged: LUCIFER, smiling, and SON of SATAN, smiling, hold the Crown of Thorns, whips and a Reed. They give these to LONGINIUS. CAIAPHAS, "mocking," covers face with hands, but peeks through fingers to watch JESUS being scourged. They strike JESUS forty times. CLAUDIA turns head away, unable to watch. JUDAS is horrified. VERONICA & WOMEN of JERUSALEM, turn heads away. Remaining CAST react. PONTIUS PILATE, alternately, seems pleased & frightened. LUCAS & TWO GUARDS enjoy striking JESUS. CORNELIUS, with growing reluctance, strikes JESUS; ANGELS bow & raise their arms outward as if to "bless" JESUS for strength. At the fortieth strike, LONGINIUS raises & then lowers his right hand, commanding it to stop. LUCAS throws Whip on ground & spits at JESUS, who with great dignity, stares at LUCAS, then collapses to ground. ANGELS, with arms outstretched, kneel toward JESUS; SATANS "flash" a self-satisfied smile. LONGINIUS warns LUCAS gesturing: "Stop!" CAIAPHAS, raising fist, gestures: "Yes!" JUDAS shoves CAIAPHAS & gestures: "This was not what I wanted. How could you!" CAIAPHAS snickers at JUDAS. MARY buries her head in her hands. JOHN the APOSTLE & MARY MAGDALENE console MARY. CLAUDIA slaps PONTIUS PILATE across face, then hands a white linen Towel to MARY.)

NARRATOR: When our hearts reach utter Darkness, God provides a glimpse of Light...through the compassion and understanding from the most unexpected of sources. *(CLAUDIA apologetically looks at MARY.)*

NARRATOR: Claudia Procles knew well Mary's pain. The blood of Claudia's nephew was needlessly spilled. Yes, Claudia's nephew was one of the Holy Innocents, some thirty years ago. *(CLAUDIA, intently, looks toward the WOMEN of JERUSALEM)*

NARRATOR: Claudia saw the mother of her dead nephew standing in the crowd.

(As CLAUDIA exits, LUCIFER hands the Red Cloak & Crown of Thorns to LONGINIUS. LUCAS raises JESUS to his feet, forcing JESUS to face the Audience.)

NARRATOR: Rather than being concerned to do what was right, Pontius Pilate wanted the blood-thirsty crowd to make his decision. He then shouted:

VOICE of PONTIUS PILATE: "LOOK at the man! I find no case against him!"

NARRATOR: But the crowds shouted: "Crucify him! Crucify Him!"

(LONGINIUS places Red Cloak upon JESUS; as he does; LUCAS grabs the Crown of Thorns & jams it onto JESUS' head. CORNELIUS sympathetically looks upon JESUS. TWO GUARDS, laugh at JESUS & then mockingly bow before JESUS. SON of SATAN hands Reed to LUCAS. LUCAS, laughing, uses Reed to strike JESUS over the head. LUCAS & TWO GUARDS spit at JESUS. ANGELS rise & "angel flake" JESUS, as a "sign" of administering strength to endure. PONTIUS PILATE stares at JESUS, then addresses Audience. LUCIFER bows before PONTIUS PILATE.)

NARRATOR: *(As ANGELS "angel flake" JESUS.)* Pontius Pilate cared more about public opinion than about what is right and moral. And so Pilate shouted:

VOICE of PILATE: "Take him away...and CRUCIFY HIM YOURSELVES!" *(PILATE exits. SATANS make a victory leap, ANGELS shudder. JUDAS slaps CAIAPHAS who laughs & exits. LONGINIUS directs CORNELIUS & LUCAS to shove JESUS. GUARDS strike JESUS as they take Him. MARY, using white linen, bends down & wipes JESUS' spilled blood. MARY MAGDALENE assists her. JOHN the APOSTLE, cries; VERONIC comforts JOHN the APOSTLE. MARY raises her blood-covered hand toward Audience.*
MARY, staring at her blood-soaked hand rises to her feet. JUDAS, approaches MARY. JOHN the APOSTLE, angrily pushes JUDAS away. JUDAS, with regret, looks back at MARY & then bows head. JUDAS then exits, interacting with Audience.

VOICE of JUDAS: "I didn't know they would do THIS to Jesus. THIS WASN'T SUPPOSED TO HAPPEN TO JESUS!" *(JUDAS, pausing, looks upward to the Heavens)* "WHY ME, GOD? WHY AM I THE ONE WHO HAS TO GO THROUGH THIS?"

BLACKOUT

(Lights still out. ETHAN, LONGINIUS, LUCAS, LUCIFER, carrying a Sword, MRS. SATAN, SON of SATAN, DAUGHTER of SATAN, as cross is placed in stand at center. THIEF crucified on Cross at one side, JOHANNA, MARY, JOHN the APOSTLE, MARY MAGDALENE, & VERONICA below cross.)

SCENE 17   ETHAN THE CROSSMAKER

NARRATOR: Standing nearby was a childhood friend of Jesus, named Ethan.

(LIGHTS UP: ETHAN starts down aisle.)

NARRATOR: As a baby, Ethan visited Jesus while He lay in the manger...only then, Ethan was held in the hands of Johanna, his mother. Johanna, also, was among the crowd.

(JOHANNA scoffs at LONGINIUS.)

NARRATOR: Johanna also was present among the crowd.
(LONGINIUS whistles. JOHANNA amorously watches LUCAS.)

NARRATOR: LONGINIUS, the Head Centurion, began his military career with the slaughter of the Holy Innocents. *(LONGINIUS searches Audience.)*

NARRATOR: Thirty some years ago...somehow...in his pursuit to kill, LONGINIUS overlooked the little manger in Bethlehem, where the Angels protected Mary, Joseph and the Infant Jesus. He also overlooked Johanna and her infant son, Ethan who were visiting the manger that night. Miraculously, their lives were spared.

(LONGINIUS, points to ETHAN, orders LUCAS to bring ETHAN to him. LUCAS grabs ETHAN by the shoulders, and forces him down aisle to LONGINIUS. JOHANNA becomes visibly upset.)

NARRATOR: LONGINIUS' son, Lucas, was a mirror image of his father. And, today, as if it were thirty-some years ago, LONGINIUS, with his son, Lucas, and with the assistance of a man named, Ethan, participated in the murder of another Holy Innocent, whom LONGINIUS overlooked thirty-some years ago.

(MARY stares at ETHAN as she goes to the altar. ETHAN, reaches out to MARY. JOHN the APOSTLE, MARY MAGDALENE & VERONICA join MARY. JOHN protectively places arms around MARY'S shoulders &, with VERONICA, escorts MARY away. As they exit, MARY MAGDALENE slaps ETHAN. LONGINIUS & LUCAS laugh. MARY MAGDALENE runs to MARY, JOHN & VERONICA.)

NARRATOR: Somewhere, along the way, Ethan decided that he would no longer worship God. *(JOHANNA admiringly looks at LONGINIUS.)*

NARRATOR: Ethan became angry at God when, while still in school, Ethan's mother, Johanna, decided to pursue her own pleasures. *(JOHANNA knowingly gazes upon LONGINIUS, pushes his shoulder in a "let's get-a-move-on" manner & seductively laughs. ETHAN, with great disgust, watches JOHANNA.)*

NARRATOR: Mary's husband, Joseph, taught Ethan the fine art of shaping wood. As an adult, Ethan's carpentry skills became a handsome-paying occupation: Ethan became an official CROSSMAKER for the Roman Empire.

(JOHANNA admiringly looks at LONGINIUS, points to ETHAN & LUCAS; she then exits to left front. LONGINIUS approaches ETHAN.)

NARRATOR: LONGINIUS gave Ethan an unwelcome order; an order which would definitely ruin his Passover holiday.

(LONGINIUS holds up three fingers before ETHAN'S face. ETHAN shakes his head "No!")

NARRATOR: LONGINIUS ordered Ethan to immediately produce three crosses. *(ETHAN holds up two fingers to LONGINIUS.)*

NARRATOR: Ethan knew that, back at his shop, he only had two, not three crosses made.

(LONGINIUS, still holding up three fingers, exits. LUCAS, holds up three fingers in ETHAN'S face, then exits. ETHAN, perplexed, steps to Center. LUCIFER, carrying a Sword, approaches ETHAN.)

NARRATOR: Then, Satan gave Ethan the notion that he should re-cycle his crosses, something which Ethan had never done.
(LUCIFER bends down to whisper into ETHAN'S ear.)
NARRATOR: Lucifer whispered to Ethan, that because it was Passover, no one would notice if Ethan stole back one of his crosses.

(LUCIFER places his arm on ETHAN'S shoulders and walks with him to the THIEF hanging on a Cross. The THIEF, with eyes closed, is still alive & breathing heavily.)

NARRATOR: Lucifer urged Ethan to steal back this cross. *(THIEF'S eyes open wide)* But, Ethan shook his head in disgust, and said:

VOICE of ETHAN: This isn't any good, that rotten thief is still alive! He's the one who robbed my shop!

(The THIEF looks fearfully at ETHAN & shakes his head. LUCIFER hands Sword to ETHAN.)

NARRATOR: But, Lucifer slyly urged:

VOICE of LUCIFER: "Here, finish him off! No one will see you…and he's going to die anyway!"

(LUCIFER places Sword into ETHAN'S hand. MRS. SATAN, SON & DAUGHTER of SATAN stroke his hand which holds the Sword. ETHAN looks around to see if anyone is watching, then, nods "Yes!" to SATANS. ETHAN aims Sword as he approaches THIEF.)

NARRATOR: Then Ethan yelled to the Thief:

VOICE of ETHAN: I NEED THE CROSS!

(SATANS guide ETHAN'S hand to stab the THIEF. THIEF shakes head: "NO!" ETHAN plunges Sword into THIEF. SATANS laugh, guide ETHAN'S hand to twist Sword into THIEF'S body. THIEF dies.)

NARRATOR: When no one hears, nor sees life come to an unnatural end, it becomes easy to kill.

(ETHAN withdraws Sword, & begins to shake as he walks away. SATANS, laughing, remain in front of THIEF on Cross & clap as ETHAN throws Sword to ground.)

NARRATOR: From that moment, Ethan believed he had placed one foot in Hell.
                              BLACKOUT

NARRATOR: When we welcome evil into our life, be prepared for its consequences.

                    MUSICAL INTERLUDE, INTERMISSION

(Lights still out. JUDAS, holds Pouch filled with 30 silver Coins, & CAIAPHIS is Center. SATANS, all hold Nooses.)

SCENE 18   JUDAS' DEATH

NARRATOR: Judas, like Ethan, felt that he had stepped into Lucifer's domain.

(LIGHTS UP: JUDAS, with great anger & disgust, throws silver Coins at CAIAPHAS who laughs sadistically. CAIAPHAS exits. As CAIAPHAS exits, SATANS sneak up on JUDAS)

NARRATOR: (As SATANS approach JUDAS.) Evil knows no boundaries; and to achieve its goals, evil will get rid of anything that stands in its way. (SATANS display Nooses to JUDAS. LUCIFER dangles Noose before JUDAS' eyes. JUDAS, runs to exit, crying.)

NARRATOR: Judas could not forgive himself for the demons of his betrayal.

(SATANS, on "tip-toes & dangling Nooses," surround JUDAS. LUCIFER lowers Noose in front of his face. SATANS swing Nooses. JUDAS raises hands to reject Noose.)

NARRATOR: Judas, like anyone who makes a grave mistake with those they love, could not forgive himself. (LUCIFER places Noose on JUDAS.) And, Judas, mistakenly, thought he could not be forgiven by God. (SON of SATAN, discarding Noose, teases JUDAS).

NARRATOR: It is thought that Judas could not forgive himself for having been abused as a child.

(DAUGHTER of SATAN, discarding Noose, approaches JUDAS; she wickedly smiles before taking & then petting JUDAS' hand.)

NARRATOR: It also has been said that Judas, himself, was a child abuser.

(LUCIFER & MRS. SATAN hug SON & DAUGHTER: SATANS laugh & gesture "Loser" sign to JUDAS' face. SATANS, facing JUDAS, laugh, gesturing "Loser" sign, and exit. JUDAS shakes with fear.)

NARRATOR: Judas would not allow the Light of Christ to touch his pain.

(JUDAS, with Noose still around his neck, walks down aisle; he interacts with Audience with a "Please help me" gesture. JUDAS stops & holds the end of the Noose high. his head turns sideways, his eyes roll & his tongue hangs out from his mouth.)
BLACKOUT

NARRATOR: *(During BLACKOUT)* In a putrid spot, Judas hung himself from a tree. It is believed that after his death, Judas' body burst open...spewing his entrails. SOUND EFFECTS: CROWS

NARRATOR: It is also said that Black Birds of prey were seen feasting upon Judas' entrails.

BRIEF MUSICAL INTERLUDE

(Lights still out. ETHAN, holding a large wooden Cross, is between TWO GUARDS. PONTIUS PILATE, holding Sign, MARY, MARY MAGDALENE, JOHN the APOSTLE, JOHANNA & ANGELS at left, CAIAPHAS, carrying Rose Petals, LUCIFER, MRS. SATAN, carrying a Handkerchief, SATANS, YOUNG BOY, holds a Water Dish, CLAUDIA, wearing a Cape, with a Hood hiding her face, at right. JESUS, LONGINIUS, CORNELIUS, LUCAS, SIMON of CYRENE, holding a Basket of Eggs, RUFUS, VERONICA, with a Sash about her waist & wearing a Veil whose inside material bears Imprint of JESUS' face, & VERONICA'S SON at Center)

SCENE 19   JESUS BEARS HIS CROSS

NARRATOR: *(During BLACKOUT)* To satisfy the crowd, Pontius Pilate had a sign made. *(LIGHTS UP. ETHAN, holding Cross, & TWO GUARDS at Front of altar PONTIUS PILATE gives Sign to GUARD. ETHAN suspiciously watches PONTIUS PILATE & GUARD.)*

NARRATOR: The sign, Pilate had made, mocked Jesus. On it was inscribed the words: "This man claimed to be King of the Jews."

(TWO GUARDS read Sign...as they do, CAIAPHAS approaches them. ETHAN, seeing CAIAPHAS, shudders. CAIAPHAS scoffs as he reads Sign.)

NARRATOR: Evil loves to make fun of any goodness that Jesus accomplishes.

(CAIAPHAS grabs & throws Sign to ground. CAIAPHAS, disgusted, exits. TWO GUARDS carry Cross to Center. LUCIFER slithers, retrieves SIGN;/exits)

NARRATOR: Whenever we defame the reputation of others, we wrongly place crosses on their shoulders.

(LONGINIUS pushes JESUS down aisle. As JESUS goes, LUCAS spits at & clubs JESUS across the back LONGINIUS signals CORNELIUS to strike JESUS; CORNELIUS hesitantly does so. At ½ way down aisle, LUCAS, laughing, hits, then trips JESUS; who stumbles forward & falls. Cross falls to ground.)

SOUND EFFECT: (Cross hitting ground. A YOUNG BOY runs down aisle to JESUS.)

NARRATOR: A young boy came running to Jesus. He wanted to soothe Jesus' pain by offering some water.

(YOUNG BOY presents Water to JESUS; who, nodding in gratitude, receives Water Dish. LUCAS, snickering, knocks Water Dish from JESUS' hands. YOUNG BOY runs off. As YOUNG BOY exits: ETHAN stares at JESUS, as if ETHAN had seen a ghost. TWO GUARDS, carry Cross to JESUS. LONGINIUS commands CORNELIUS & LUCAS to force JESUS to stand. They shove Cross onto JESUS' shoulder. JESUS, using one arm, steadies upper Cross. ANGELS stretch arms towards JESUS.)

NARRATOR: As Jesus' hands embraced the wood of the Cross, He must have recalled the numerous hours he spent in Joseph's carpentry shop, whittling wood, lovingly, freely; never expecting that, one day, pieces of wood would be used to whittle him. (ETHAN, recognizing JESUS, shakes his head: "NO!" TWO GUARDS, laughing, beat JESUS to move down aisle. As JESUS approaches Center, He falls to ground under the Cross.)

SOUND EFFECT: (Cross hitting ground.)

(After SOUND EFFECT: LUCAS kicks & spits at JESUS. LONGINIUS strikes JESUS, directs CORNELIUS to strike JESUS; CORNELIUS, hesitantly, strikes JESUS across the back. MARY runs to assist JESUS.)

SCENE 20   MARY

NARRATOR: *(As MARY runs to JESUS)* What was on Mary's mind that day, as She watched Her Son being led to His execution on a Cross, that was made by Jesus' friend.

(MARY pauses/ angrily stares at ETHAN, then helps JESUS to stand.)

NARRATOR: Surely, Mary must have asked Herself: "Why would my son, Jesus, be condemned as a common criminal, especially when all he ever did was help people live better lives?"

(LUCAS, snickering, slaps MARY'S hand away from JESUS. JOHN the APOSTLE & MARY MAGDALENE approach MARY. MARY slaps LUCAS across the face. LUCAS, looking pleased, sneers at MARY, LONGINIUS & GUARDS, but not CORNELIUS, laugh.)

NARRATOR: Yes, as parents have to do, Mary had the tough love; the courage, to intervene when her child's life was in the wrong hands. (JESUS, embracing Cross on shoulder, slowly stands. MARY, with great love, looks into JESUS' face, then places her arm across JESUS' shoulder. ETHAN, shamefully, bows his head. MARY & JESUS walk to "Golgotha." MARY uses her Veil, wipes JESUS' forehead. CORNELIUS sneers at JESUS & MARY. LONGINIUS, LUCAS & TWO GUARDS raise their hands as if to tear MARY & JESUS apart. ANGEL MICHAEL, drawing Sword, approaches LONGINIUS. MARY MAGDALENE & JOHN the APOSTLE beg MARY to leave. ANGEL RAPHAEL places his arms as if to protect MARY'S shoulders. ETHAN, wishing to apologize, approaches MARY. ANGEL GABRIEL bows before MARY.)

NARRATOR: Ethan saw Jesus' blood that painted Mary's hands. He also could not ignore the pain that consumed Mary's heart.

(ETHAN genuflects, begs forgiveness from MARY.)

NARRATOR: Ethan was now ashamed that he was using the skills— which Mary's husband, Joseph, taught him—to help kill Jesus—his childhood friend.

(JOHN the APOSTLE punches ETHAN. ANGEL RAPHAEL "chuckles." ANGEL GABRIEL, nodding disapproval, approaches JOHN the APOSTLE; who raises his hand to strike ETHAN again. MARY raises hand & gestures to

JOHN: "Stop!" JESUS gestures "No more." JOHANNA, stridently, approaches MARY; MRS. SATAN, follows JOHANNA. ETHAN, glares at JOHANNA.)

NARRATOR: Johanna stepped forward...as if to apologize to Mary for the behavior of her son, Ethan. However, Johanna was covering up her own failure to love.

(JOHANNA hugs MARY. MRS. SATAN mocks JOHANNA'S "sincerity.")

NARRATOR: Parents have no need to apologize for the lives of their adult children. Instead, parents need to allow their adult children to rise or fall by themselves.

(JOHANNA cries on MARY'S shoulder. MRS. SATAN, pretending to "blow her nose into a Handkerchief," exits. MARY MAGDALENE, sensing hypocrisy, motions for JOHANNA to leave.)

NARRATOR: Parents need to always love their children...even when they do not love their children's actions.

(JOHANNA slaps ETHAN, then exits. LONGINIUS & LUCAS wave JESUS forward. JOHN the APOSTLE hugs MARY, then places his arm across her shoulder; JOHN bids MARY to leave. MARY, accompanied by JOHN the APOSTLE & MARY MAGDALENE, reaches out to JESUS.)

NARRATOR: Yes, we need to love our children...even when we are powerless to help them.

(JESUS reaches out to MARY; LONGINIUS & LUCAS beat JESUS. ANGELS, raising hands in Blessing, assemble in an "arc" formation behind JESUS. JOHN the APOSTLE covers MARY'S eyes. He & MARY MAGDALENE "escort" MARY to exit.)

NARRATOR: We need to accept...to be able to love ourselves...especially, during those times, when we want to help our children...but are prevented from doing so by forces beyond our control.

(LONGINIUS, "stares down" the Audience, then claps his hands: ordering CORNELIUS to "scout" the Audience. ANGEL RAPHAEL and LUCAS keeping a distance, follow CORNELIUS. SIMON of CYRENE & RUFUS coming down aisle, ANGEL RAPHAEL, bowing & with outstretched arms towards SIMON, remains near JESUS.)

SCENE 21   SIMON OF CYRENE

NARRATOR: Simon of Cyrene was a pagan who, accompanied by his son, Rufus, desired to sell his eggs at Market. In town for a profit, Simon never thought that others would profit from his expense. *(LUCAS incites CORNELIUS to "grab" SIMON.)*

NARRATOR: The Guards forced Simon to help Jesus carry His Cross.

(LUCAS "kick-backs" SIMON; who...trying to save Eggs, raises Basket up. RUFUS retrieves Basket. CORNELIUS shoves SIMON down aisle. SIMON, falls to ground. LUCAS snatches Basket & shoves RUFUS away. LUCAS reaches into Basket, takes an Egg, begins tossing it in the palm of his hand & then throws Egg & Basket to ground. RUFUS kicks LUCAS, LUCAS shoves RUFUS. CORNELIUS raises SIMON to stand.)

NARRATOR: Even though Simon had no religious affiliation, he loved to hear Jesus preach. However, Simon was too afraid to become a disciple of Jesus.

(LONGINIUS directs CORENLIUS & LUCAS to bring SIMON before JESUS; RUFUS follows. SIMON, stands before JESUS, studies the pain in JESUS' face. LUCAS strikes SIMON. LONGINIUS directs CORNELIUS to lift the end

of JESUS' Cross. LUCAS forces SIMON to place his shoulder under the Cross. CORNELIUS drops Cross onto SIMON'S shoulder. ANGEL RAPHAEL, extends hands out, blessing SIMON.)

NARRATOR: Simon never thought that he would become Jesus' helper.

(LUCAS spits at SIMON. RUFUS, making a fist, strikes LUCAS' back & kicks LUCAS' legs. LUCAS snarls at SIMON, as if saying: "Your kid is a pathetic brat!")

NARRATOR: In the future, Simon's son, Rufus would become a disciple of Jesus. Rufus saw that his father, Simon, initially was reluctant to carry Jesus' Cross.

(ANGEL RAPHAEL "angel flakes" SIMON & then retreats. LONGINIUS commands JESUS & SIMON to carry Cross. RUFUS walks alongside SIMON; CENTUTIONS & GUARDS accompany them.)

NARATOR: But, God the Father filled Simon's heart with grace, to accompany every step Simon took, under the weight of the Cross.

(JESUS & SIMON, carry the Cross)

NARRATOR: Sometimes, the moments when we are hesitant to help others, become incredible moments of miraculous grace.

(LUCIFER incites LUCAS to club RUFUS. RUFUS, groaning, falls to ground. SIMON, drops end of Cross, lunges toward LUCAS. LUCAS snarls. CORNELIUS holds SIMON in place. SIMON, helpless, reaches out to RUFUS. JESUS, still carrying Cross, extends hand in "Blessing." LONGINIUS slaps JESUS' hand. CORNELIUS, with great sadness, looks at JESUS. SIMON & LUCIFER begins to slowly applaud, bows to LUCAS then

retreats right. As LUCIFER retreats: VERONICA'S SON runs to the fallen RUFUS. VERONICA, anxiously, follows SON down aisle.)

SCENE 22   VERONICA & HER SON

NARRATOR: At any age, we can comfort one another. *(VERONICA'S SON assists RUFUS to stand. Young hearts, like the friend who ran to help Rufus, do not know the fear of the aged. Following the friend was his mother, whose name is SERAPHIA. VERONICA approaches altar, pauses & looks, with great concern, at JESUS.)*

NARRATOR: SERAPHIA was present at the marriage of Mary and Joseph. SERAPHIA is better known by the name "Veronica."

(VERONICA hugs SON.)

NARRATOR: Years ago, Veronica lost her only child during Herod's slaughter of the Holy Innocents. Veronica, with her husband Sirach, adopted this young boy nine years ago. *(VERONICA kisses SON'S forehead.)* And, as Jesus walked to Calvary, VERONICA also took it upon herself to adopt JESUS' pain.

(LONGINIUS orders CORNELIUS & LUCAS to place Cross on SIMON'S shoulder. They beat JESUS & SIMON. VERONICA seeing GUARDS' cruelty motions for SON to step back & wait. VERONICA kneels before JESUS. CORNELIUS suspiciously looks at VERONICA; LONGINIUS & LUCAS become amused as they watch VERONICA.)

NARRATOR: VERONICA remembered the day Jesus healed her hemorrhaging…and now Veronica lovingly desires to do everything…that was in her power…to stop the flow of Jesus' blood.

(VERONICA removes Veil, then uses Veil to wipe JESUS' face. ANGELS GABRIEL, MICHAEL & RAPHAEL, bow in gratitude; SATANS play "air fiddles

in mock sympathy," JESUS, with face still covered by Veil, swoons as if greatly refreshed. CAIAPHAS, pretending tears, tosses Rose Petals on JESUS & VERONICA. JESUS removes Veil from face, smiles, gratefully nods, hands Veil back to VERONICA; who looks at Veil, then kisses it. MRS. SATAN, gesturing as if cat's claws were scratching a post, snatches VERONICA'S Veil, throwing it into air. MRS. SATAN wildly laughs & watches Veil fall upon ground. VERONICA'S SON attempts to take Veil; LUCAS, sneering, prevents it.
LONGINIUS, looking bored, orders CORNELIUS to make VERONOICA depart. As he does, CLAUDIA, with Hood covering most of her face, approaches VERONICA. JESUS, seeing CLAUDIA, smiles. SIMON of CYRENE watches VERONICA & CLAUDIA. RUFUS, afraid, hugs SIMON of CYRENE.)

NARRATOR: Claudia Procles was a secret friend of Veronica. Yes, Pontius Pilate's wife, in disguise, entered the scene.

(LUCIFER, sniffing the air like a dog, approaches CLAUDIA; CAIAPHAS is not sure who this Woman is, CLAUDIA stares into JESUS' face & whispers "thank you." JESUS nods "your welcome." CLAUDIA places her arm around VERONICA'S shoulder & gestures: "We should leave."

NARRATOR: Often, Claudia, in disguise, would go and listen to Jesus. She witnessed many of His miracles…especially when Jesus brought a Centurion's child back from the dead. Claudia desired to become a Christian.

(LUCAS, impatiently shoves VERONICA away from JESUS. LUCIFER & MRS. SATAN laugh. ANGEL RAPHAEL raises arms, to form a protective umbrella, over VERONICA. VERONICA'S SON cries. ANGEL RAPHAEL gently pushes VERONICA to Front of altar. JESUS, as if to say "thank you," extends hand outward to VERONICA. SATANS & CAIAPHAS gesture "Loser" sign towards VERONICA, then exit. CLAUDIA urges VERONICA to wipe

tears from SON'S eyes & hug SON; who then turns toward JESUS. ANGEL RAPHAEL exits. LONGINIUS orders CORNELIUS & LUCAS to adjust Cross on JESUS & SIMON'S shoulders & make JESUS & SIMON take a few steps forward at Top Center...RUFUS attempts to help by trying to left/hold the bottom of Cross. VERONICA'S SON runs back, toward JESUS, retrieves Veil & looks at it with wonder. VERONICA'S SON lifts Veil high, showing the Imprint of JESUS' face to Audience.)

Voice of VERONICA'S SON: Today, when someone is sick or in need of cheer, we send flowers or cards. During Jesus' time, it was customary to give a veil, like Veronica's, to cleanse the patient's face. *(VERONICA'S SON, still holding Veil high with Imprint toward Audience)* This practice would become what's known as the "Prayer Shawl Ministry," an expression of sympathy, compassion and prayerful support.

(VERONICA'S SON gives Veil to VERONICA; she & CLAUDIA stare at Imprint on Veil. VERONICA looks back & throws "air kiss" to JESUS.)

BLACKOUT

NARRATOR: Veronica never expected that Jesus would give a gift in return.

(Lights still out. VERONICA, SON, & CLAUDIA go to left. DISMAS, carrying Cross, with GUARD carrying Whip, & GESTAS, carrying Cross, with GUARD carrying Whip, to Center. Remaining CAST stays in place from last scene.)

SCENE 23   THIEVES: DISMAS & GESTAS

NARRATOR: On Good Friday, two thieves were crucified with Jesus. One was known as DISMAS, the Good Thief.

(LIGHTS UP. DISMAS, carrying Cross, & GUARD, carrying Whip, start down aisle.)

NARRATOR: Some thirty years ago, DISMAS, was about the same age as Veronica's first son. At that age, DISMAS became friends with an older child. Unfortunately, DISMAS allowed this *older child to badly influence him. The older child's name was GESTAS.*

(DISMAS pauses, then regretfully looks Back. GUARD whips DISMAS, who drops Cross to ground. GUARD again whips DISMAS & orders him to pick up Cross.)

NARRATOR: DISMAS allowed GESTAS to challenge him to commit a crime, that of robbery. Their attempted victims were four Wise Men, who were travelling to Bethlehem in hope of honoring a new-born King.

(GUARD pushes DISMAS toward Center. GESTAS, carrying Cross, & GUARD, carrying Whip, start down aisle.)

NARRATOR: GESTAS was known as the Bad Thief. It was GESTAS' idea to rob Mary and Joseph, as they fled from Bethlehem with the Baby Jesus. However, DISMAS would not allow GESTAS to complete this crime.

(GESTAS pauses, snarls & flexes his Bicep for Audience. GESTAS then snarls at GUARD. GUARD whips GESTAS; who squints eyes & makes no other reaction.)

NARRATOR: GESTAS never appreciated the hard work of his parents. He wanted more than they could provide. His only belief was in the evil of ultimate selfishness. *(GESTAS flexes Bicep)* GESTAS never believed that life could be transformed. His anger blinded him, as would a crow who plucked out his eyes as he hung upon his cross.

(GUARD, whips & then commands GESTAS to Center, DISMAS & GUARD go to left.)

NARRATOR: DISMAS had no one, in his life to show him what was good and true. He always wanted a role model to follow, but, was too lazy to acknowledge one.

(GUARD, laughing, whips DISMAS; who falls. GUARD pulls DISMAS up. GUARD, laughing, whips GESTAS; who throws Cross to ground & punches GUARD. GUARD & GESTAS fight. LUCIFER, laughing & applauding, approaches GESTAS.)

NARRATOR: DISMAS was present when Jesus delivered His Sermon on the Mount...and he enjoyed the free loaves and fish that Jesus provided for lunch. DISMAS believed that Jesus could show him a better way of life, but DISMAS was afraid to approach Jesu and ask for help. *(ANGEL MICHAEL "angel flakes" DISMAS for strength.)*

BLACKOUT

(Lights still out. SAMARITAN WOMAN, SOFIA, carrying BABY, CLAUDIA, carrying white linen Towel & wearing Cape & Hood, CONRAD, bearing Sword & Pouch with medicinal Herbs at Center, JOHANNA, ETHAN, TIRA, WOMEN of JERUSALEM), at left. GESTAS' MOTHER, carrying a Jug of "spirits," DISMAS, carrying Cross, and GUARD go to (l) of altar; GESTAS, carrying Cross, & GUARD go to (r) of altar. MARY, MARY MAGDALENE, JOHN the APOSTLE, & VERONICA at left. Remaining CAST: {LUCIFER & MRS. SATAN carrying Coins, CAIAPHAS carrying Handkerchief, CENTURIONS & GUARDS bearing Swords, stay in place)

SCENE 24   WOMEN OF JERUSALEM

NARRATOR: *(During BLACKOUT)* Walking along the way with Jesus, were Women who lamented Jesus' suffering. Some of them were mothers of the Holy Innocents. They, too, had endured the shocking loss of a child. These women were grieving for Mary as well as for themselves. Despite their pain, some of the women were also open to whatever future Blessings...second chances...that God and His Angels would deliver.

(LIGHTS UP, LONGINIUS orders CORNELIUS & LUCAS to beat JESUS & SIMON; CORNELIUS is hesitant. RUFUS kicks CORNELIUS; LUCAS laughs. SAMARITAN WOMAN starts down aisle. SIMON, dropping Cross, punches LUCAS. LONGINIUS "strong-arms" & then throws SIMON to ground. LUCAS orders SIMON to take Cross. RUFUS hugs SIMON. LUCAS, malevolently, snickers at SIMON & RUFUS.)

NARRATOR: Yes, Second Chances, like the time Jesus meet this Samaritan Woman at Jacob's well. She had multiple failed marriages. Yet, Jesus accepted her for who she was.

(SAMARITAN WOMAN, approaches altar. GESTAS spits at her. SAMARITAN WOMAN pauses to wipe spit off. LUCIFER gives: "thumbs-up" to GESTAS; GUARD laughs. SAMARITAN WOMAN slaps GESTAS, then goes to JESUS.)

NARRATOR: Jesus knew the Samaritan Woman's need to be understood, forgiven and valued. Jesus gave her the very Blessing of True, Chaste, Love...and, she would forever testify how Jesus helped her.

(JESUS extends arm outward & greets SAMARITAN WOMAN; who bows head & kneels. TIRA approaches DISMAS.)

NARRATOR: DISMAS' Mother, TIRA, regrets the fact that she never knew her son's friends. If she did, TIRA never would have let DISMAS befriend GESTAS.

(TIRA stares at DISMAS who is about to cry. TIRA turns away from DISMAS, glares at GESTAS; who sticks his tongue out at TIRA. MRS. SATAN applauds TIRA. ANGEL RAPHAEL places hands, as if Blessing, over DISMAS.)

NARRATOR: TIRA always told DISMAS that he was a disappointment to her. And DISMAS, in his heart, felt that his mother had disappointed him.

(TIRA bows her head towards JESUS. She raises her head and angrily stares at LONGINIUS; who looks as if he saw a ghost.)

NARRATOR: TIRA heard that Jesus was in Jerusalem; she also heard that Jesus was able to heal broken hearts. TIRA, not concerned about the pain of her son, determined to bring her pain to Jesus for healing.

(GESTAS' MOTHER, guzzling "spirits" from Jug, staggers to altar.)

NARRATOR: Yes, all children have possibilities to achieve dreams...as well as the possibilities for Good...as well as for Evil. So do their parents. *(GESTAS' MOTHER belches.)*

SOUND EFFECT: BELCHING

(GESTAS' MOTHER uses Jug to salute Audience, then holds Jug high as if Jug were the Torch on the Statue of Liberty.)

NARRATOR: GESTAS' Mother saluted everything and everyone in her life. *(GESTAS' MOTHER guzzles contents of jug.)* She wanted to wish Jesus well. After all, Jesus gave her free bread and fish on the day He delivered His Sermon on the Mount.

(LUCIFER stands behind GESTAS' MOTHER; who, still holding Jug, uses other hand to accusingly point finger at Audience.)

NARRATOR: GESTAS' Mother then shouted:

VOICE of GESTAS' MOTHER: "What's the matter with all of you? *(She points at JESUS.)* He gave us free food! And you're stringing him up on the Cross?" *(She points finger at Audience. MRS. SATAN, gesturing: "Shish," approaches GESTAS' MOTHER; who stands, on "rocky feet," before her son, GESTAS. SATANS, gleefully stand behind GESTAS.)*

NARRATOR: Then, she shouted to her son, GESTAS:

VOICE of GESTAS' MOTHER: "Not like you, you pathetic waste! You never did anything nice for your Mother! But, it's not too late to redeem yourself. Surely you pick-pocketed one of these guards! Give me some money! I need a refill!"

(GESTAS' MOTHER, still holding Jug, begins to frisk GESTAS; finding no money, she raises her hand "in dismissal" at GESTAS.)

NARRATOR: Right then, GESTAS'' Mother thought.

(GESTAS' MOTHER looks as if a Light Bulb just lit inside her brain)

VOICE of GESTAS' MOTHER: Jesus did that Miracle at Cana with the wine; surely He can refill my Jug!

(GESTAS' MOTHER "snaps" to attention, then hurriedly kneels & holds up Jug to JESUS, who looks at her with great love, then shakes His head in disbelief.)

NARRATOR:) Yes, like GESTAS' Mother, many only go to God as a last resort.

(GESTAS' MOTHER, puts her head in her hands, "fakes" a sympathetic cry of affectation, then peeks up at JESUS. LUCAS, and the others, in disgust, look at GESTAS' MOTHER; in a "please, please, please help me fashion," raises her hands upward to JESUS.)

NARRATOR: Decisions made by parents do leave a lasting impression upon their children...even when they think their children don't notice.

(GESTAS shakes his head at MOTHER, then stares at ground. SATANS scoff & gleefully rub hands together. SOFIA, carrying BABY, walks down aisle)

NARRATOR: Often, parents wrongly believe that it is too late for their children, or for themselves to improve.

(SOFIA, carrying BABY, approaches altar.)

NARRATOR: A woman from Jerusalem, named Sofia was also present that day. Sofia had allowed herself to be used by GESTAS.

(ANGEL RAPHAEL, with outstretched arms as if to comfort, approaches SOFIA.)

NARRATOR: Sofia once believed that GESTAS really loved her.

(SOFIA slaps GESTAS across face. GESTAS smiles: "liking" the slap.)

NARRATOR: GESTAS did not love Sofia for her mind or for her heart. In fact, Sofia allowed herself to be taken by any male who gave her attention.

(GESTAS snickers at SOFIA.)

NARRATOR: Sofia's father never acknowledged, nor had time for her.

(SOFIA, shielding BABY, bows and presents BABY to JESUS. LUCAS, gestures: "C-R-A-Z-Y! LONGINIUS is amused. CORNELIUS sadly looks upon BABY RUFUS huddles against SIMON. JESUS, looking with great love upon SOFIA & BABY, bids her to rise.)

NARRATOR: Sofia acknowledged that Jesus did have time for her. (WOMEN of JERUSALEM approach JESUS.)

NARRATOR: Jesus had counseled Sofia. He helped her realize and believe that she, indeed, was a beloved child of God. Sofia came to thank Jesus for restoring her dignity and worth.

(SOFIA smiles at & then kneels before JESUS. WOMEN of JERUSALEM kneel to SOFIA'S (r) & (l); they extend hands, as if in praise, towards JESUS.)

NARRATOR: Yes, in a male-dominated society, Jesus radically preached that women were the equal of men…that women were to be loved and respected…as one should love and respect oneself. *(JOHANNA approaches altar)* Yet, some parents, like Johanna, fail to respect themselves. As they grow older, so does their shame, their guilt, for not giving their children their time, interest, direction. After all, a child's behavior is learned from their parents' example; or lack thereof. *(JOHANNA, pretending to be "in control," inspects Audience.)*

NARRATOR: As Johanna aged, she grew bitter with herself.

She filled herself with guilt over the care and attention she should have given her son, Ethan.

(LUCIFER, MRS. SATAN, SON of SATAN, & DAUGHTER of SATAN, applaud & stand behind JOHANNA.)

NARRATOR: Johanna knew that she had failed to introduce Ethan to more faith. *(SATANS raise hands in a "V" for victory formation.)* Johanna knew that she should have been more grateful for the Blessing that Ethan's life was spared when he was an innocent baby. *(SATANS gesture: "thumbs-up!" JOHANNA turns around and glares directly at SATANS.)*

NARRATOR: Johanna realized that she had forgotten God once she got what she wanted from Him.

(JOHANNA, like a "drama-queen" with open arms, approaches JESUS. SATANS, sticking fingers into mouth as if to regurgitate, go to altar.)

NARRATOR: But, today, Johanna wanted one thing more; she wanted to hear Jesus say that her "sins were forgiven."

(LUCAS pushes JOHANNA backward, preventing her from approaching JESUS. JOHANNA waves a disapproving finger at LUCAS who sneers at JOHANNA with a "Lady, bite me" look.)

NARRATOR: *(As LUCAS pushes JOHANNA backward.)* Sadly, Johanna waited too long to ask Jesus for forgiveness.

(ETHAN goes to assist JOHANNA, who gratefully hugs him. JOHANNA & ETHAN go to (l). CLAUDIA, wearing Cape with Hood, & holding a white linen Towel, starts down aisle.)

NARRATOR: There were many men and women that were healed by Jesus. It was a shame that only these few came to comfort Jesus in His time of need.

(As CLAUDIA approaches JESUS, MRS SATAN, sticking foot out, trips CLAUDIA, who falls to ground, the white linen Towel gets tossed into air & then lands on ground.)

NARRATOR: But, sometimes, others do not want to see anyone else be healed.

(As CLAUDIA falls upon ground, JOHANNA shoves ETHAN to CLAUDIA.)

NARRATOR: Sometimes, people make themselves look better than they are; they take advantage of others' misfortune. And, when they do, this type of person will try to keep the spotlight upon them.

(JOHANNA regains composure, "finger combs" her hair, takes a deep breath & with a self-satisfied look, turns her head up to JESUS; who rolls His eyes.)

NARRATOR: Johanna is like the quintessential "phony person" at a funeral service...who only attends the funeral because of the free meal.
(ETHAN assists CLAUDIA to rise. CAIAPHAS, "salivating," on "tip-toes" to altar & turns to Audience, in mock sympathy, blows his nose into handkerchief. LUCIFER, approaches LONGINIUS, gestures: "GET the WOMEN OUT of HERE!" GUARDS push WOMEN away; WOMEN, with arms stretched towards JESUS, go to (r) & (l). LONGINIUS orders CORNELIUS & LUCAS to adjust Cross upon JESUS' & SIMON'S shoulders. LUCAS strikes SIMON & JESUS. RUFUS, angry, is ready to kick LUCAS; who gestures: "don't you dare try". DISMAS, with great love, steps forward to meet JESUS; GUARD hits DISMAS. GESTAS laughs; GUARD beats GESTAS. LONGINIUS then orders JESUS & SIMON to go to proceed. RUFUS tries to help carry bottom of Cross. As JESUS, SIMON, RUFUS carry Cross they walk between WOMEN. JESUS, with great sympathy, looks to WOMEN.)

NARRATOR: In varied ways, Jesus reached out and touched the hearts and souls of these women. Jesus' example empowers us to never underestimate our ability to reach out, if only to touch.

SCENE 25   JESUS' GREAT FALL

(WOMEN, with outstretched arms, turn toward JESUS, SIMON & RUFUS; who approach altar. The SAMARITAN WOMAN follows. LONGINIUS & LUCAS strike at JESUS & SIMON. CORNELIUS motions for WOMEN to stay back. JESUS wavers under weight of Cross. ANGELS "angel flake" JESUS & then retreat. GESTAS' MOTHER approaches LONGINIUS; raises Jug & gestures: "I need money." LONGINIUS slaps GESTAS' MOTHER to move away.)

NARRATOR: The Roman Guards had no respect for women, children…or life at all. The Centurions and Guards are like family members who experience great delight when relatives…brothers, sisters, the ex-wife, the ex-husband, favored son or favored daughter…crash and burn…especially when their pedestal has been quite tall.

(LUCAS beats JESUS to move faster; LONGINIUS clubs SIMON across the back. LUCAS, like an out-of-control warrior, "clubs" JESUS below the knees, causing JESUS to collapse. The Cross hits, with a loud noise, to ground. SOUND EFFECT. SAMARITAN WOMAN, hysterical, reaches out to JESUS & then falls on knees. SIMON & RUFUS run to & try to help JESUS rise: JESUS, as if dead, remains on ground. ANGELS, holding hands outward in Blessing, approach JESUS. SATANS, laughing & gesturing: "Loser", approach ANGELS. LUCAS wildly laughs. LONGINIUS, with remorse, looks upon JESUS. CORNELIUS, angry, gestures: "Keep your lips shut" to LUCAS.)

NARRATOR: Yes, at times, even the best families crash and burn; a fall from grace, from the seemingly perfect marriage, from the apparently wonderful job, the foreclosure of a house repossession of a car, the filing for bankruptcy; the fall from dignity, popularity or fame. Yes, even the most faithful person can be like the rose: after the petals blossom and fall, only the thorns remain.

(SIMON, thinking JESUS dead, rises: RUFUS, frightened, holds onto SIMON. SATANS pull SIMON'S arm; gesturing: "You belong with us!" ANGELS approach SIMON & pull on SIMON'S right arm, gesturing: "NO! YOU'RE WITH US!" ANGELS & SATANS continue tugging at SIMON as if splitting him in two.)

NARRATOR: When we fail the hardest...good and evil pull at us the hardest.

(LUCAS strikes SIMON; SIMON collapses. RUFUS, crying & thinking SIMON dead, lies down on SIMON'S body. LUCAS spits on SIMON & RUFUS. SATANS laugh; ANGELS shudder. ANGEL RAPHAEL places hand upon RUFUS' shoulder. ETHAN shoves LUCAS upon the chest. SATANS retreat)

NARRATOR: ETHAN, the Crossmaker was not known for his courage. Yet, even spineless Ethan could not tolerate Lucas' blatant disregard for life. ETHAN shouted:

VOICE of ETHAN: "WHAT'S WRONG WITH YOU, KILLING ANOTHER INNOCENT PERSON? YOU KILLED HIM IN FRONT OF HIS SON! YOU'RE NOTHING BUT A SENSELESS COWARD!"
(LUCAS, insulted & "snorting" at ETHAN, raises Sword.)

SCENE 26   CONRAD—the FOURTH WISE MAN

(JOHANNA covers ETHAN'S mouth; then pulls ETHAN backward. LUCAS spits at ETHAN & JOHANNA & then upon JESUS. LONGINIUS kicks JESUS to see if He is still alive. SATANS, carrying Jugs of "spirits," distribute Jugs to LONGINIUS, CORNELIUS & LUCAS: who click Jugs together as if making a toast, then drink. LUCAS drinks from Jug until dry & then tosses Jug away as he approaches JESUS.)

NARRATOR: Lucas mocked Jesus shouting:

VOICE of LUCAS: "YOU DON'T LOOK VERY KINGLY NOW! GET YOURSELF UP!"

(MARY, with JOHN the APOSTLE & MARY MAGDALENE following, slaps LUCAS: MARY then points finger at LUCAS.)

VOICE of MARY: DON'T YOU DARE TOUCH MY SON AGAIN!

NARRATOR: But Lucas smirked,

VOICE of LUCAS: "Let's get real, Lady! I can't wait to strip & nail him dead! We'll see who's King around here!"

(MARY slaps LUCAS' face. SATANS wince; ANGELS applaud. JOHN the APOSTLE & MARY MAGDALENE pull MARY back)

NARRATOR: However, the Guards did not know that there was another King in town that Good Friday. This King's name was Conrad. *(CONRAD parades down aisle)*

NARRATOR: Some thirty years ago, Conrad traveled with the Three Wise Men to Bethlehem. There, at the innkeeper's manger, Conrad gave the Infant Jesus a Golden Statue in the shape of an Angel.

(SATANS, forming hands into "Periscopes," step into Center Aisle & stare at CONRAD'S approach.)

NARRATOR: Conrad noticed that ever since that Epiphany day, he never seemed to age. Conrad forever searched for Jesus, because he wanted to thank Jesus for this gift of eternal youth.

(MARY and CAIAPHAS, looking very disturbed step into Center Aisle)

NARRATOR: Mary recognized Conrad and remembered his kindness.

(MARY greets CONRAD; they embrace. LUCIFER, looking at CONRAD & MARY, waves "OH NO!" CAIAPHAS, hissing like a snake, at CONRAD, slaps LUCIFER & gestures: "DO SOMETHING!" MARY & CONRAD go to JESUS. LUCAS, intently, watches CONRAD.)

NARRATOR: Conrad never thought that such a kindly King, as Jesus, would be treated like this.

(CONRAD takes Pouch of medicinal Herbs & attempts to anoint JESUS; but LUCAS, drawing Sword, stops CONRAD.)

NARRATOR: Conrad wanted to anoint Jesus' wounds with his medicinal herbs. But, Lucas would not let him.

(CONRAD draws Sword. JOHN the APOSTLE escorts MARY to left, MARY MAGDALENE embraces MARY. SIMON, seeing a duel about to start, shields RUFUS who continues to hug SIMON. CONRAD & LUCAS duel: LUCAS' Sword flies to ground. CONRAD points Sword at LUCAS' heart, but allows

LUCAS to live. CONRAD proceeds to use Herbs to anoint JESUS. LUCIFER whispers into LUCAS' ear; LUCAS draws Sword & impales CONRAD. LUCAS, smiling, withdraws Sword. CONRAD, mortally wounded, turns & looks at LUCAS.)

VOICE of CONRAD: "Why? I let you go free."

(CONRAD stumbles forward & dies with dignity. LONGINIUS & CORNELIUS take a desperate drink from Jugs.)

BLACKOUT   MUSICAL INTERLUDE

(Lights still out. JESUS' Cross is placed on floor in Front of altar; Crosses for DISMAS & GESTAS are placed into their stands at right & left. JESUS, LONGINIUS, CORNELIUS, carrying three pieces of Rope, & LUCAS, with Dice, at Center, GESTAS, GUARD, holding Rope, SATANS, holding Staffs & carrying large Nails, & CAIAPHAS, holding Sign, at right, DISMAS, GUARD, holding Rope, ANGELS, VERONICA, VERONICA'S SON at left, MARY, MARY MAGDALENE, & JOHN the APOSTLE are near foot of JESUS' Cross: SIMON of CYRENE & RUFUS stands to their (r) & JOHANNA, ETHAN stand to their (l). TWO YOUNG CHILDREN at Back. Remaining CAST stands (r) & (l) of altar.)

SCENE 27   STRIPPING of JESUS' GARMENTS

NARRATOR: (During BLACKOUT) There is good stripping, and there is bad stripping in our lives.

(LIGHTS UP. GUARD strips GESTAS, who flaunts his physique, & pushes GESTAS to CROSS.)

NARRATOR: (As GESTAS flaunts his physique.) The Bad Thief, GESTAS, to his very end, stripped himself of any goodness.

(GESTAS, pumping up his chest, spits at GUARD face; GUARD slaps GESTAS, then begins to rope GESTAS' arms to Cross.)

NARRATOR: *(As GUARD ropes GESTAS to Cross)* While on the cross, GESTAS mocked Jesus...demanding that Jesus produce an instant miracle. GESTAS missed out on the miracle that was his...free for the asking...if only he didn't reject Jesus. *(GESTAS, as if possessed, sticks his tongue out at GUARD.)*

NARRATOR: The Good Thief, DISMAS, was also stripped of his garments.

(GUARD strips DISMAS, looking humiliated, & pushes him to Cross. DISMAS, as if he were a "puppy without a home, looks at GUARD.)

NARRATOR: But DISMAS would not strip himself of this last opportunity to recognize Jesus' goodness. *(DISMAS, stretching his entire body, looks heavenward.)*

NARRATOR: DISMAS silently made a Prayer of Trust.

(GUARD ropes DISMAS' arms to Cross: DISMAS continues to look upward, his face "beams" as if soaking in Light. ANGEL GABRIEL approaches the back of DISMAS' Cross.)

NARRATOR: From his prayer, DISMAS received the courage...while hanging on the Cross...to ask Jesus for a place in His Heavenly Kingdom...unlike Judas...whose sole interest was in an earthly Kingdom. While being crucified on Calvary, DISMAS became Jesus' disciple. He is the Patron Saint for anyone who receives the Death Sentence.

(GUARD punches DISMAS. SATANS, stomping Staffs into ground, then point Staffs, as if a rifle about to be fired, at JESUS. LUCIFER raises & then lowers Staff. LONGINIUS & CORNELIUS strip JESUS' Garment.)

NARRATOR: The Guards stripped Jesus of His garments…as the cloth was ripped away from Jesus' flesh, it, once again, tore open the wounds marks across His chest and back.

(LONGINIUS throws JESUS' Garment into air. CORNELIUS attempts to retrieve Garment as it falls upon ground. LUCAS stops CORNELIUS. LUCAS displays Dice to CORNELIUS & throws Dice to ground. LUCAS wins &, like a rabid dog, grabs Garment & swirls Garment in victory! LUCAS then wraps Garment about his waist. MARY runs to JESUS & kneels at His feet. MARY MAGDALENE & JOHN the APOSTLE try to comfort MARY. JESUS, looking upon MARY, places His hand on her shoulder; MARY looks upward at JESUS. CORNELIUS, with great empathy, looks upon MARY.)

NARRATOR: Mary's heart was like that of every parent… whose heart and soul know well the words of Jesus' Beatitudes: "Blessed are you when they insult you, and utter every kind of evil, falsely, against you, because of me."

(LONGINIUS shoves JESUS. MARY, MARY MAGDALENE & JOHN the APOSTLE follow MARY. ANGELS MICHAEL & RAPHAEL place their hands on MARY'S shoulders, LONGINIUS points to the Cross & throws JESUS down near Cross. LONGINIUS commands LUCAS to bring SIMON to JESUS. LUCAS slaps SIMON, and. RUFUS kicks LUCAS' leg. LUCAS snarls at RUFUS & then "roughhouses" SIMON. As LUCAS forces SIMON to altar, ETHAN followed by JOHANNA, approaches JESUS)

NARRATOR: Then, Ethan the CROSSMAKER ran towards Jesus pleading:

VOICE of ETHAN the CROSSMAKER: Jesus, I have done something terribly wrong!

(LUCAS attempts to push ETHAN back. ETHAN punches LUCAS & then, bending down whispers into JESUS' ear.)

NARRATOR: Ethan bent down and whispered in Jesus' ear.

VOICE of ETHAN: "I don't know if I can ever be forgiven...I purposely killed a man... *(ETHAN begins to cry)* ...because I wanted to reuse his cross." *(JESUS looks into ETHAN'S eyes.)*

NARRATOR: And, in a faint voice, Jesus asked:

VOICE of JESUS: "Do you wish to be forgiven?"

NARRATOR: Ethan then told Jesus that the Cross he recycled is the Cross that Jesus is carrying. Jesus looked at Ethan...with great love...as He said:

VOICE of JESUS: "Go and kill no more. I forgive you."
(JOHANNA berates ETHAN.)

NARRATOR: Ethan's mother, Johanna, became impatient. She scolded Ethan *(JOHANNA "twists" ETHAN'S ear.)* and told him that his behavior may cause them to be late for their Passover Celebrations.

(SATANS, display Nails, approach JESUS, then stand, laughing; holding Nails over JESUS. CAIAPHAS, displaying Sign, approaches JESUS, snickering, holding SIGN high for Audience to see. SATANS & CAIAPHAS gleefully look at each other & make an affirmative nod. LONGINIUS taking JESUS' right arm, CORNELIUS, taking JESUS' left arm & LUCAS, taking JESUS' feet, stretch JESUS onto Cross.)

VOICE of JESUS: WILD GROANS

(LUCAS approaches MARY; removes JESUS' Garment & flaunts Garment in MARY'S face. VERONICA slaps LUCAS. LUCAS, stunned, regains composure. VERONICA & SON hug MARY.)

BLACKOUT

(Lights still out. JESUS, stretched upon Cross. LONGINIUS, CORNELIUS & LUCAS hold Hammers & Nails high. SATANS, each, hold a Jug of "spirits" for LUCIFER who holds two Jugs. CAIAPHAS holds Sign high as if a winning delegate at a Convention.)

NARRATOR: *(During BLACKOUT)* Many miracles are said to have occurred during Jesus' Crucifixion. In the 17th Century, a Spanish nun, Mary of Agreda, who was a mystic, recounted that when the soldiers turned over the Cross, with Jesus' Body nailed to it; Angels made the earth open, to prevent Jesus' body from being smashed into the ground. Mary Magdalene is said to be a witness to this miracle. Another miracle also occurred during Jesus' Nailing, with a whole crowd of witnesses.

SPECIAL EFFECTS: FOG

SCENE 28   NAILING

NARRATOR: *(During BLACKOUT)* Jesus' Body radiated with intense pain. Before grabbing his mallet to nail Jesus to the Cross, Cornelius, the Assistant Centurion, remembered that Jesus had raised his child from the dead.

(LIGHTS UP: DAUGHTER of SATAN hands Jug to CORNELIUS. CORNELIUS, putting down Hammer & Nail, drinks heavily.)

NARRATOR: To numb his guilt, Cornelius drank profusely…and so did the other guards.

(LUCIFER distributes Jugs to LONGINIUS & LUCAS, who put down Nails & Hammers; MRS. SATAN & SON of SATAN distribute Jugs to TWO GUARDS by THIEVES. Upon receiving Jugs, CENTURIONS & GUARDS hold Jug high, then freely drink)

SPECIAL LIGHTING: (As CENTURIONS & GUARDS drink from Jugs.)

NARRATOR: Satan made certain that their bottles would never run dry.

(LUCIFER slaps LONGINIUS' shoulder. LONGINIUS puts Jug down & then drunkenly whistles.)

SOUND EFFECT: "LOOPY" WHISTLE BLOW

(Upon whistle: CORNELIUS, LUCAS & TWO GURADS put Jugs down. They grab Nails & Hammers, position Nails upon JESUS' hands & feet; then raise Hammers to strike. LONGINIUS prepares to whistle for Hammers to be lowered; ETHAN frantically runs to CAIAPHAS.)

NARRATOR: ETHAN the Crossmaker shouted:

VOICE of ETHAN: "They never used nails to crucify criminals on my crosses before! WHY are you using Nails, TODAY!? Why aren't you using ropes?"

(CAIAPHAS belly-laughs & snorts like a pig; LUCIFER gives ETHAN a side-head slap…like: "hello?" LUCAS laughs at ETHAN & then motions to LONGINIUS: "Let's get a-move-on!")

NARRATOR: Lucas, the Younger Centurion wanted to get the job done as quickly as possible…he wanted to go to the Sea of Galilee and celebrate the holiday with his friends.

(DAUGHTER of SATAN approaches LUCAS & nudges his Hammer downward. LUCAS, looking at LONGINIUS, slightly lowers Hammer. DAUGHTER of SATAN kisses LUCAS' cheek.)

NARRATOR. With time, Lucas became desensitized to killing. Sadly, he even came to enjoy it.

(LONGINIUS, raising fingers to mouth, begins to whistle.)

SOUND EFFECTS: "LOOPY" WHISTLE BLOW

(ETHAN, with arms flying, tries to stop LUCAS from hammering. LUCAS, using Hammer, strikes ETHAN on side of head.)

VOICE of ETHAN: STOP! YOU CAN'T DO THIS! JESUS DID NOTHING WRONG!"

(ETHAN staggers i& falls dead to ground. LUCAS snickers & spits on ETHAN. JOHANNA, wailing, runs to ETHAN.)

(SOUND EFFECTS: (VOICE of JOHANNA, WAILING; MARY places her hands, as if in Blessing, over ETHAN. ANGEL RAPHAEL, with outstretched arms, also Blessing ETHAN.)

NARRATOR: Despite her own pain, Mary…the quintessential Mother…reached out to help…to heal the pain of another.

(ETHAN rises from the ground. JOHANNA embraces ETHAN. JOHN the APOSTLE embraces MARY. CENTURIONS, drop Nails & Hammers; GUARDS, take Jugs, heavily drink & begin to stagger. CAIAPHAS &

SATANS seethe with anger. ANGEL MICHAEL, raises Sword, to protect MARY.)

NARRATOR: Never underestimate the intercession of a Loving Mother. It is said that many miracles, which are not recorded in Scripture, also came from Mary's love that day.

BLACKOUT

(Lights still out. MARY between JOHN the APOSTLE & MARY MAGDALENE at Cross. MRS. SATAN, holding BABY wrapped in swaddling clothes, stays out of sight. LONGINIUS, CORNELIUS & LUCAS have Nails on JESUS' hands & feet; they raise hammers before striking Nails into JESUS'S flesh).

SPECIAL EFFECTS: FOG
SOUND EFFECTS: HAMMERING /NAILING

NARRATOR: *(During BLACKOUT)* There is a prayer called: "The Silent Prayer of Nailing." Whenever we are in situations beyond our control, simply open the palms of our hands, exposing ourselves to whatever is about to happen, and trust in God's providential care.

(After 10—12 hammer strikes: LIGHTS UP, with strobe. LONGINIUS, CORNELIUS, LUCAS continue to Nail JESUS to Cross. JESUS writhes with pain. MARY, near fainting, reaches out to JESUS. GESTAS laughs; GUARD slaps GESTAS.)
DISMAS, shuts eyes and prays; GUARD mocks GESTAS' prayer. MRS. SATAN, holding BABY, offers BABY, in mockery, to MARY.)

NARRATOR: Taking advantage of Mary's pain, Mrs. Satan drew near and tempted Mary:

VOICE of MRS. SATAN: "I have my baby safe in my arms...why isn't your child safe, too? Did God the Father forget about you? Ha! Ha! Ha! Ha HAH!"

(ANGEL MICHAEL, drawing Sword, forces MRS. SATAN to retreat. JOHN the APOSTLE & MARY MAGDALENE comfort MARY.   Hammering/Nailing continues. CAIAPHAS, holding Sign, gleefully hands Sign to DAUGHTER of SATAN; she gives Sign to LONGINIUS. LUCAS, while hammering, watches LONGINIUS who reads sign, looks at CAIAPHAS, puzzled, & gestures, "Why did you write this?" CAIAPHAS snickers. & gestures: "I wrote this?" LUCAS throws Hammer down, in frenzied manner, grabs Sign & proceeds to nail Sign to upper Cross.)

NARRATOR: The sign placed on Jesus' Cross mocked Jesus, with the title: "He claimed to Be King of the Jews."

(LUCIFER, wearing a King's Crown, laughs & "struts" before MARY.)

NARRATOR: Our jealousies, and petty grievances, often hammer insults upon those we love, and should cherish.

BLACKOUT

SOUND EFFECTS: CREEPY LAUGHTER

(Lights still out. Cross set in stand at Top Center. JESUS stands crucified on Cross/JESUS' hands are also roped to Cross. JESUS is between LONGINIUS, with Spear & flask & CORNELIUS. LUCAS stands by CORNELIUS. Nearby are SIMON & RUFUS. THIEVES' Crosses set in stands at (r) & (l) of JESUS. GESTAS is on Cross at (r). GUARD stands to (r) of Cross; SATANS & CAIAPHAS stand near. DISMAS is on Cross at (l) of altar. GUARD stands to (l). ANGELS are near. Jugs of "spirits" are on ground near SATANS. A Sponge is near LONGINIUS. MARY, JOHN the APOSTLE, MARY MAGDALENE, VERONICA & SON, JOHANNA & ETHAN

at left. *ANGELS GABRIEL, MICHAEL & RAPHAEL stand behind MARY.*
WOMEN of JERUSALEM, CHILDREN & CAST kneel before crosses with
hands upraised.)

SPECIAL EFFECTS: FOG

SCENE 29   CRUCIFIXION

NARRATOR: *(During BLACKOUT)* It is believed that the ancient
Philistines started the practice of executing criminals by crucifixion.
They started the practice of hammering nails through the bundles of
nerves which connected to the criminals' fingers and toes. Any
movement that Jesus made with His hands and feet would cause
excruciating pain. And, anyone who was crucified on a Cross had to
frequently move up and down, in order to breathe. Jesus had to push
and pull Himself up, numerous times, to capture the slightest passages
of air. Crucifixion was a cruel and slow death which lasted two, three,
four, even five days. Death usually came from thirst, the loss of blood,
or suffocation.
(LIGHTS UP). JESUS, looking upward, breathes heavily. His chest
heaves in pain; His stomach collapses inward. JESUS' entire body
writhes in shock.)

SPECIAL EFFECTS: STROBE   SOUND EFFECTS: (Throughout
entire scene) THUNDER   LIGHTENING

VOICE OF JESUS: "Father, forgive them, for they do not know what
they are doing."

(DISMAS, painfully stretching his body to look toward JESUS, nods: "You're
right." A sense of serenity overcomes DISMAS' face & the strained muscles of
his torso seem to relax. DISMAS sighs)

NARRATOR: DISMAS heard Jesus praying for those who mutilated Him. In that instant, DISMAS knew that Jesus was the type of Messiah he was searching for. This moment of redemptive grace, of redemptive hope, gave DISMAS' spirit new life.

VOICE OF JESUS, as JESUS looks at DISMAS;. "Truly I tell you, today, you will be with me in paradise."

(DISMAS, further stretching to look at JESUS, nods: "Thank you!" MARY, crying, runs to Cross & kneels JOHN the APOSTLE runs after & by MARY. JESUS looks down at MARY.)

VOICE of JESUS: "Woman, here is your son."

(MARY begins to cry. JOHN the APOSTLE embraces MARY & then wipes her tears. JESUS looks at JOHN.)

VOICE of JESUS: "Here is your Mother."

(JESUS, gasping for air & breathing heavily & chest expanding & heaving outward, stretches his neck to look to Heaven.)

VOICE of JESUS: "My God, My God! Why? Have You forsaken Me?"

(JESUS' body begins to quiver. CORNELIUS, in fearful awe, "studies" JESUS. LONGINIUS readies Spear & "practice aims" Spear at JESUS. JOHANNA stares at LONGINIUS. LUCAS, yawning, looks at his fingernails. GESTAS scoffs & sticks tongue out at JESUS. DISMAS intently watches JESUS & repeatedly looks upward to Heaven.)

NARRATOR: As Jesus hung on the Cross, Johanna stared at LONGINIUS, the Head Centurion. Suddenly, she realized why this older Centurion looked so familiar.

(As JOHANNA approaches LONGINIUS; he stays his Spear. JOHANNA points finger at LONGINIUS' face.) NARRATOR: Johanna shouted at LONGINIUS.

VOICE of JOHANNA: "You're that brut! Thirty-some years ago, I met you, in Bethlehem, at the Innkeeper's Manger! You may not remember, but, you spared Jesus' life. *(JOHANNA points to JESUS)* He was the Infant born in the manger, and I was there, too, with my Infant son, Ethan, your Crossmaker!"

(LONGINIUS, as if hit by confusion, stares at ETHAN, then JESUS, then JOHANNA, then at MARY. JOHANNA slaps LONGINIUS across the chest.)

VOICE of JOHANNA: The Angels protected us. You looked at all of us as if you didn't see us! *(JOHANNA, falls to ground on knees & then raises hands together as if praying)*

VOICE of JOHANNA   You can't take Jesus' life today! Please! Please don't!

(LONGINIUS, squinting, studies JOHANNA, then shakes his head: "No!" LUCIFER, holding Jug of "spirits" slithers to LONGINIUS.)

NARRATOR: LONGINIUS, the Head Centurion, did not readily recognize Johanna. Ever since he slaughtered the Holy Innocents, LONGINIUS' sight began to fail, *(LONGINUS rubs his eyes.),* especially during the past several years.

(LUCIFER taps LONGINIUS on shoulder, & then holds out Jug to him.)

NARRATOR: As LONGINIUS studied Johanna's face; he recalled that six days ago, he saw Jesus heal a blind youth.

(LONGINIUS, turns to LUCIFER, grabs Jug & guzzles "spirits." LUCIFER, as if wearing an imaginary hat, "tips" hat toward JOHANNA, & then, smiling, slithers right.)

NARRATOR: LONGINIUS regretted that he, too, did not step forward to ask Jesus to restore his sight.

(LONGINIUS tosses Jug to ground & wipes mouth dry. His whole body begins to quiver, he looks up.)

NARRATOR: Yet, despite his failing eyesight, LONGINIUS did notice that the sun was about to eclipse.

VOICE OF JESUS: "I thirst."

(LONGINIUS takes Sponge, places it on Spear, and pours "spirits" on Sponge. LONGINIUS holds up Sponge to JESUS' lips. JESUS sways head "NO!" LUCIFER strikes GESTAS across the chest. GESTAS, "growls" at LUCIFER.")

NARRATOR: Satan continued to operate through GESTAS; he taunted:

VOICE of LUCIFER: "Look around, everyone is running away, they're abandoning you. There will be no one left."

(LUCIFER again strikes GESTAS.)

NARRATOR: Lucifer whispered these same words to Jesus when His disciples abandoned Him in the Garden at Gethsemane.

(ANGELS GABRIEL, MICHAEL, RAPHAEL, with arms held outward, as if to embrace a loved one, kneel before JESUS; ANGELS raise hands up as if they were transporting JESUS to Heaven.)

VOICE of JESUS: "Father, it is Finished."

(JESUS looks upon MARY; who raises her hands, lovingly looks up at Him. JESUS' body convulses. He stretches His head to Heaven.)

VOICE of JESUS: "Father, into Your hands I commend my Spirit."

(JESUS convulses, bows His head and dies. ANGELS bow & lie prostrate on ground. Others comfort MARY and each other. LONGINIUS readies his Spear. The apostles and LONGINIUS, look at JESUS' dead body. CORNELIUS guiltily stares at MARY. LUCAS, angry, impatient, tries to take Spear.)

NARRATOR: Sometimes, we are propelled into the horrible choice of maintaining life, or ending it.

(MARY MAGDALENE & VERONICA urge MARY to leave. MARY gestures: "NO!" ANGELS stretch hands out to MARY. JOHN the APOSTLE helps MARY to stand. MARY, still held in JOHN the APOSTLE'S arms, exits. ANGELS, MARY MAGDALENE & VERONICA follow MARY. JOHANNA stares at LONGINIUS & then at LUCAS before exiting. TWO ANGELS, who remain, "keep guard" on JESUS' body on Cross: ANGELS kneel. LUCAS roughly grabs Spear from LONGINIUS, who turns to LUCAS & nods: "Yes...Just do it." LUCAS aims spear at JESUS' body, JOHANNA, rising, waves: "NO!" LONGINIUS gestures to LUCAS: STOP!" LUCAS, livid, throws Spear at LONGINIUS feet. GESTAS demonically laughs.)

SOUND EFFECT: LAUGHTER

NARRATOR: Unfairly, life horribly drops us. We are forced to make decisions where no one will win.

NARRATOR: Like Lucas, the Young Centurion, sometimes we have to give up; give back; even when our jobs, our families, our friends demand that we enter into situations where we know we should not go.

(LONGINIUS retrieves Spear, his hand shaking; he goes into mad rage, points Spear, in threatening manner, at WOMEN of JERUSALEM; WOMEN panic & exit. LONGINIUS drinks from Flask & then, holding up Flask & Spear, offers them to audience. LONGINIUS snaps to attention, turns to face the crosses, then, as if a Knight in a Jousting Tournament, aims Spear at JESUS, and plunges it into JESUS' side. BLOOD & WATER flow out. As LONGINIUS withdraws Spear: he "jerks' his head backward, as if struck. He drops Spear to ground & raises hands to wipe his eyes.)

SPECIAL EFFECTS: BLOOD (on LONGINIUS' hands)

NARRATOR: Blood and water flowed from Jesus' side.

NARRATOR: *(As LONGINIUS wipes his eyes)* Jesus' blood & water also splashed across LONGINIUS' face and eyes.

(ANGEL RAPHAEL gently places hand upon LONGINIUS' eyes; then retreats. LONGINIUS stares at Audience, smiles, looks up at JESUS, then gratefully stares at Heaven, saying: "Thank You!" LONGINIUS, kneels before JESUS' Cross & removes Helmet. SATANS rage: MRS. SATAN slaps LUCIFER, who slaps DAUGHTER & SON. CORNELIUS places hand on LONGINIUS' shoulder. CORNELIUS turns his head away from JESUS & stares upon ground. LUCAS sneers at LONGINIUS & CORNELIUS.)

NARRATOR: Slowly, this Head Centurion realized that he, like Ethan, was the recipient of another miracle, LONGINIUS' eyesight was perfectly restored.

NARRATOR: (As LONGINIUS kneels & removes Helmet) But, as LONGINIUS' eyesight grew bright...the sky grew dark...and the earth began to quake.

(As LUCAS sneers at LONGINIUS, SON of SATAN retrieves fallen Spear, but LUCAS places his foot on Spear. LUCAS wickedly smiles, then removes foot from Spear. SON of SATAN, hissing at LUCAS, takes Spear & hands it to GUARD. SATANS, applauding, gather around GESTAS on Cross. GESTAS, demonically, sticks out tongue. GUARD aims Spear at GESTAS' body, & impales him. SATANS mock: "OOPS!" As GESTAS dies, his face contorts into an expression of anger. GUARD, using Spear, breaks GESTAS' bones at hands & feet. CAST responds. LUCIFER grabs Spear from GUARD & "prances" over to GUARD by DISMAS on Cross; DISMAS, sensing evil, shudders & then raises his eyes to Heaven; his body, despite pain, "flexes" to regal attention. LUCIFER hands Spear to GUARD; holding Spear, takes a few steps back, aims Spear at DISMAS' body, then plunges Spear into DISMAS. SATANS, gleefully, jump up & down. GUARD withdraws Spear. DISMAS' face exhibits great pain & then great peace as he dies. SATANS look at DISMAS with disgust. CAST responds. TWO ANGELS, keeping "guard," rise to feet & bow to JESUS.)

SOUND EFFECTS: LOUD THUNDER & LIGHTENING

BLACKOUT

NARRATOR: Jesus died to save all sinners. He died so that all would know of God the Father's immense love for His Creation. That even when we sin...purposefully turning away from God's love...Jesus' life shows us that it is the goal of God the Father that all people be happy...during our temporary stay on earth...and then forever in Heaven. If we close our mind and heart to Christ, we will never know the fullness of God's Love.

(Lights still out. THIEVES remain crucified on Crosses. JESUS' Cross, {without JESUS' body} with Sign still attached, remains upright in stand. JUDAS is between ANGEL MICHAEL & LUCIFER. They tug at JUDAS' arms as if each wants JUDAS all for themselves.)

SCENE 30   JUDAS IN HELL

   SPECIAL EFFECTS: FOG   STROBE
SOUND EFFECTS: LIGHTENING   THUNDER

NARRATOR: No one can hide from the truth. It is believed that Jesus, after His death on the Cross, descended into Hell to free souls…giving them a second chance…if they wanted. And, when Jesus did…Judas…once again… had to face the truth.

(LIGHTS UP. JUDAS tries to free himself from LUCIFER'S grasp, but LUCIFER "yanks" JUDAS toward him.)

NARRATOR: Judas wanted to run away from Satan, *(SAINT MICHAEL pulls JUDAS toward him),* and he wanted to run away from Jesus.

(JUDAS pulls away from SAINT MICHAEL, looks at LUCIFER, who wipes his tongue across his lips, and gestures: "Come with me! You won't be sorry!" JUDAS looks at SAINT MICHAEL, who raises his Sword & gestures: "You'll be safe with me!" JUDAS, placing his hands over his ears, as if to quiet the noise in his mind, begins to cry & shake.)

NARRATOR: Judas wanted to run away from his very self. Even though Judas could not accept responsibility for his betrayal…

(ANGEL MICHAEL stands behind JUDAS, then gently places arm on JUDAS' shoulder. JUDAS shrugs & "flicks" SAINT MICHAEL'S hand from his shoulder. JUDAS walks away from SAINT MICHAEL)

NARRATOR: Jesus wished that Judas would allow himself to experience His forgiveness...

NARRATOR: But, that's the remarkable thing about God...He will not force-feed His Love.

(LUCIFER, licking his lips & rubbing palms together goes to JUDAS: SAINT MICHAEL, holding Sword out, as if a gate, stops LUCIFER.)

NARRATOR: To let our self be loved, even when we are not worthy of that love, requires genuine humility.

(JUDAS, turning around, looks at LUCIFER, who smiles & then bows to JUDAS as if saying: "I am at your service.")

NARRATOR: JUDAS rejected Jesus' love once.

(JUDAS looks at SAINT MICHAEL, who raises Sword in a "knightly" salute & then opens his arms in welcome.)

BLACKOUT

NARRATOR: Did Judas reject it again? We'll find out that answer, when each of us makes our eternal journey.

MUSICAL INTERLUDE

(LIGHTS still out. MARY sits, holding JESUS' dead body. MARY is surrounded by JOHN the APOSTLE, ETHAN, JOHANNA, MARY MAGDALENE, VERONICA & SON, holding Herbs bottles of spirits. JOSEPH of ARIMATHEA, SIMON & RUFUS, hold Burial Cloth, surrounded by ANGELS. CAIAPHAS & SATANS, holding Pitchforks & Jugs of "spirits," on opposite side. DISMAS & GESTAS remain crucified; GUARDS, holding dirty Burial Cloths, stand by them. WOMEN of JERUSALEM, TIRA, SAMARITAN

WOMAN, SOFIA & YOUNG CHILDREN, stand holding Flowers. Flowers are placed on altar. A Basket, filled with brightly colored Eggs & covered with a Cloth, is "planted" in Center Aisle. Three Nails, used to crucify JESUS, on floor by JESUS' Cross.)

SCENE 31   REMOVAL FROM CROSS AND BURIAL

NARRATOR: *(During BLACKOUT)* When our love is authentic, we desire what is best for our loved ones. But, can we…with tearful joy…give them back to God? Back to God Who lovingly loaned them to us…even if only for a short while? Veronica's Veil comforted Jesus' painful Face… *(LIGHTS UP. VERONICA & SON approach MARY. VERONICA sprinkles Herbs over JESUS' body: Her son, very upset, watches Herbs fall on JESUS; his hand unfolds, displaying Herbs. MARY MAGDALENE watches VERONICA.)*

NARRATOR: Once more, Veronica comforted Jesus; she veiled His Body with herbs, as was the practice, to preserve.

(MARY MAGDALENE goes to VERONICA'S SON & grabs Herbs from his hand. ETHAN, tries to intervene. MARY MAGDALENE. and VERONICA shove each other. SON kicks ETHAN. MARY looks at this "shove fest" with sadness. She runs her fingers across JESUS' Crown of Thorns. JOHN the APOSTLE stops VERONICA & MARY MAGDALENE from further shoving)

NARRATOR: Many times, at Funerals, families argue over who does what…or gets what. Passages in the Old Testament remind us that there is a right time and a right place for everything. We should not disrespect the dead with self-centered, insensitive behavior which only shines Light on the Darkness of our petty jealousy and insecurity.

(MARY, still in shock, removes Crown of Thorns from JESUS' forehead & hair, holds it up for all to see. GUARDS remove DISMAS & GESTAS from Crosses. TIRA watches as DISMAS & GESTAS, lifelessly fall upon ground.

GUARDS place Burial Cloths on the bodies, then laugh, and stomp on the covered bodies. SATANS, poke THIEVES' covered bodies with their pitchforks. MARY holds Crown of Thorns to her heart.)

NARRATOR: On their own, skeletons come out of closets at Funerals. *(TIRA bows head as DISMAS' body falls to ground; covers her eyes as GUARD stomps on DISMAS' body)* Today is one such day.

(SATANS raise Jugs to salute the dead bodies of DISMAS, GESTAS & JESUS; they guzzle "spirits." TIRA kneels by DISMAS' body, partially uncovers Burial Cloth, & strokes DISMAS' hair. LONGINIUS, seeing TIRA, looks as if he has seen another ghost.)

NARRATOR: Tradition says that the name of DISMAS' mother was TIRA. She stayed to see her son taken down from the Cross.

(TIRA covers DISMAS' head. LUCAS goes to her)

NARRATOR: TIRA was also the mother of Lucas, the "wanna-be" Head Centurion.
(TIRA raises Flowers to her nose, closes her eyes & inhales their fragrance.)

NARRATOR: TIRA never married LONGINIUS, Lucas' father.

(TIRA places Flowers on DISMAS' body. LUCAS grabs and throws Flowers to ground. TIRA, livid, rises. LUCAS stomps on Flowers. SATANS, laugh. TIRA slaps LUCAS. LONGINIUS grabs LUCAS' hand and twists his arm as he is about to slap TIRA.)

NARRATOR: LONGINIUS told his son: "Lucas, I have killed an innocent man today. Please, please don't become what I am. (LONGINIUS releases LUCAS' arm.) You're young…start your life over…it's not too late."

(LUCAS gestures "Loser!" & then runs to MARY, points toward JESUS' body.)

VOICE of LUCAS: "WHAT A WASTE!"

(TIRA slaps LONGINIUS & exits. LONGINIUS remains in place as if "frozen." MARY bows head & hugs JESUS' face. ANGELS surround MARY.)

VOICE of MARY: "Yes, young man, you have wasted your life, but, it does not have to be that way."

(MARY, with increasing sadness, looks upon LUCAS, then presses JESUS' body against her; CORNELIUS, very disturbed, strong arms LUCAS.)

VOICE of CORNELIUS: "THAT'S NO WAY to talk to this woman! She has done nothing wrong to you!" *(LUCAS attempts to free arm from CORNELIUS' hold.)*

VOICE of LUCAS: "Let me go old man! I'm sure Herod would love to hear that his Assistant Centurion is defending a criminal's mother!"

(LUCAS shakes arm free, glares at CORNELIUS' & exits, in a rage.)

NARRATOR: It is never too late for any of us. Life hands us thousands of chances to start again. All we have to do is choose one.

(JOSEPH of ARIMATHEA, SIMON & RUFUS place Burial Cloth over JESUS' body: ANGELS assist. SATANS watch. WOMEN of JERUSALEM, SAMARITAN WOMAN, SOFIA, & CHILDREN, as if forming a funeral procession, place Flowers on JESUS' body. SATANS act sick. WOMEN exit. After last WOMAN: MRS. SATAN, feigning tears, mocks MARY.)

NARRATOR: And, usually, during our deepest times of grief come the strongest temptations.

(SATANS raise Jugs as if "saluting" JESUS' dead body. SATANS "guzzle "spirits" & then belch. ANGELS, angry, wave their hands to sweep SATANS away. MARY MAGDALENE comforts MARY. ANGEL MICHAEL knocks Jug away from LUCIFER. LUCIFER, comically gestures: "All right, I get the message." ANGELS line up against SATANS as if battle is about to begin. SATANS point fingers at ANGELS saying: "Just wait, I'll get you!" SATANS retreat. GUARD tears Sign from JESUS' Cross. He presents it to MARY. ANGELS return as "Sentinels." to MARY & JESUS. JOHN the APOSTLE places arm around MARY'S shoulder)

NARRATOR: From that day on, John the Apostle did as Jesus asked, he took Mary into his care as if Mary was his own Mother. *(GUARD points to Sign & laughs. CORNELIUS shoves GUARD. GUARD gestures: "Loser," & exits. CORNELIUS stares at JESUS' lifeless body. LONGINIUS pats CORNELIUS' back. LONGINIUS, looks at JESUS, respectfully removes Helmet & genuflects).*
NARRATOR: None of us is beyond redemption, regardless of what we may have done.

(LONGINIUS places his arm across CORNELIUS' shoulder; they exit, in quiet sadness.)

NARRATOR: What beauty can we return for the beauty of loving family members?

(RUFUS presents flowers to MARY, then kisses her cheek)

NARRATOR: It is thought that Simon of Cyrene and his Son, Rufus, became Disciples.

(SIMON kisses MARY upon cheek, then hugs RUFUS. RUFUS gestures "I'm hungry," looks at Audience, searching.

NARRATOR: Rufus was hungry. He searched for something to eat.
(RUFUS points to ground & retrieves Basket of brightly colored Eggs.)

NARRATOR: To Rufus's surprise…he found that it was the same basket that he and his father were forced to leave behind. RUFUS holds Basket up to SIMOM; who appears amazed.)

NARRATOR: More surprising was that not a single egg was broken.

(RUFUS & SIMON hold up colored Eggs, while, GUARD, with DISMAS, goes to Jesus' Cross & takes Three Nails.)

NARRATOR: Only now, the eggs' shells were no longer white, the eggs' shells had miraculously become a rainbow of vivid color.

(SIMON & RUFUS, smiling, display Eggs to Audience as they exit.)
NARRATOR: Thus, the tradition of coloring eggs for Easter was born.

(GUARD, holding Three Nails, approaches MARY.)

NARRATOR: Love, and beauty are not recognized by everyone. For love and beauty threaten anyone whose purpose is to degrade.

(GUARD, snickering, tosses Nails to ground by JESUS' body, gestures: "thumbs down." ETHAN & JOHANNA, go to MARY. GUARD snarls as he exits.)

NARRATOR: Then, Ethan the Crossmaker stepped forward.
(ETHAN kneels before MARY, places his hands on her hands)

NARRATOR: He wanted to apologize to Mary. Ethan was very ashamed of the person he had become, and that Jesus had to be crucified, on a piece of wood, which had been fashioned by his hands.

(JOHANNA removes Veil & uses it to wipe MARY'S tears.)

NARRATOR: As Veronica used her Veil to wipe Jesus' face, Johanna now used her Veil to dry Mary's tears.

(JOHANNA hugs MARY. ETHAN kisses palm of his hand & places his palm on MARY'S cheek.)

NARRATOR: From the actions of these women a Tradition was born; the use of a veil, blanket or shawl to comfort and heal was the forerunner of the pall; the dignified piece of material which we place upon the casket of our beloved deceased on the day of their funeral. *(JOHANNA hugs ETHAN; as he puts his arm around her shoulders. JOHANNA approvingly looks on ETHAN as they exit).*

NARRATOR: This white funeral garment, like our Baptismal Garment, also reminds us of the comfort, and the dignity with which Jesus clothes us in eternity.

(JOHN the APOSTLE helps MARY to stand. She stares at JESUS' body. ANGEL GABRIEL goes to altar, gets a flower for MARY, and she cries. JOHN places arm around MARY. She takes, kisses the flower and raises it to Heaven. ANGELS raise arms. MARY gently drops Flower onto JESUS' body. ANGEL MICHAEL raises Sword high in salute, then exits. MARY held gently by JOHN, exits.)

NARRATOR: As Jesus' life and teachings remind us: we only need to do one thing- to love. Yes, to love as God loves. Jesus' command to love one another as we would want to be loved: so simple, and yet, so eternally hard.

(As MARY & JOHN exit: CAIAPHAS, "snidely," approaches JESUS' body: he lifts the Burial Cloth & gleefully turns toward Audience.)

VOICE of CAIAPHAS: *(laughing)*: "HE'S DEAD!" *(CAIAPHAS rubs his hands together and addresses the Audience.)*

VOICE of CAIAPHAS: *(With mock sympathy)* "Did you know that Jesus is dead?" (CAIAPHAS, laughing, exits) He's dead! He is DEAD! HE IS DEAD…DEAD…DEAD! DEAD! HA! HA! HA! HA! HA! HA!

BLACKOUT

NARRATOR: *(During BLACKOUT)* Every action taken with pure love never goes unnoticed by God. Jesus' death on the Cross tells each of us that Jesus expressed His eternal love for us, by the sacrifice of His life. Jesus wanted this so badly that He was willing to hand Himself over to the powers of Evil, to redeem sinners. Throughout the Old Testament there were predictions that the true Savior would conquer the Powers of Darkness, which introduced evil, suffering and death into the world. Only one person brought himself back to life…and walked away from the tomb. Only one person demonstrated that the powers of Darkness have no power over Him. Yes, Satan gave it his best shot. But Satan, who is the negation of all Love, never thought that the Light of total, selfless Love would be infinitely more powerful than Darkness.

(Lights still out. JESUS' Burial Cloth is draped on the crossbeam of JESUS' Cross which remains in Stand. ANGEL MICHAEL, with Sword raised high, stands to (l) of Cross. ANGEL GABRIEL stands before Cross. ANGEL RAPHAEL stands to (r) of Cross. MARY, MARY MAGDALENE, JOHN the APOSTLE, ANGELS, RUTH, THOMAS & ALTAR SERVER, enter, carrying Cup filled with Wine, & Dish with Bread. ETHAN, JOHANNA, SIMON, RUFUS, holding Basket with colored Eggs, JOSEPH of ARIMATHEA & CLAUDIA at right. THIEVES' Crosses & Stands are removed.)

SPECIAL EFFECTS: FOG

SCENE 32   RESURRECTION
MUSIC: HANDEL'S HALLELUIAH CHORUS

(On the third "Alleluia:" LIGHTS UP. JESUS enters, Center. MARY MAGDALENE & JOHN the APOSTLE enter from tomb area. ANGEL GABRIEL steps forward to MARY MAGDALENE & JOHN the APOSTLE motioning: "He is not here!" ANGEL GABRIEL opens arms to Audience, bows & points to JESUS as He enters. ANGEL GABRIEL exits. MARY MAGDALENE urges JOHN and MARY to face the tomb, MARY embraces JESUS. Together, JESUS & MARY walk down aisle. They meet MARY MAGDALENE & JOHN the APOSTLE. They raise arms in gratitude, to the Heavens. SIMON, RUFUS, holding Basket with Eggs, & JOSEPH of ARIMATHEA greet JESUS. RUFUS, with great enthusiasm shows JESUS the Basket & colored Eggs. JESUS, smiling, musses RUFUS' hair. JESUS & CAST then go to Center. JOHANNA & ETHAN greet JESUS, MARY, MARY MAGDALENE & JOHN the APOSTLE. JESUS & CAST all turn to face Cross & joyfully raise their hands in a "V" formation, smiling in gratitude to God the Father. glory! Triumphantly, JESUS leads CAST, followed by ANGELS, to Front. CAST interacts with Audience as they joyfully exit.)

SCENE 33   PRESENT DAY / FIRST COMMUNION MORNING

NARRATOR: *(As RUTH & THOMAS go to altar.)* Ruth, Thomas & family arrive at Saint Michael's Church, before the start of his First Communion Mass. Ruth showed Thomas colorful scenes from scripture. (These can be painted by students, depicted in stained glass windows, or projected on screens at the altar). *(RUTH, still holding THOMAS' hand, escorts him to Center)*

NARRATOR: Ruth then continued her answer to Thomas' question of: "Where does Evil come from?"

VOICE of RUTH: After everything I told you this morning, Thomas, there is the answer to your question: Jesus loves us so much that He gave up His life for us on the Cross. And, because Jesus rose from the dead, we know that He will always be with us, to love and forgive us;if we let Him enter our lives.

(An ALTAR SERVER, carrying Cup of Wine & Dish of Bread, enters. THOMAS closely observes as the ALTAR SERVER places the Chalice & Dish for the Eucharistic ceremony.)

VOICE of RUTH: And, that is why every Sunday is traditionally called a "Little Easter."

(RUTH hugs THOMAS, then leads him to the altar.)

VOICE of RUTH: Your First Communion Mass, and every Mass, celebrates Jesus' Passion, His dying, and rising from the Dead; just as Jesus promised at the Last Supper. He will be forever with us, especially each time we receive Him in Holy Communion.

(THOMAS smiles at RUTH, then says)

VOICE of THOMAS: Grandma, I love Jesus. I will always choose to do what is right. *(RUTH smiles, hugs THOMAS & then, arm-in-arm, they exit, LUCIFER & SATANS, pouting, move to the darkened corners of the sanctuary. LUCIFER points an accusatory finger at Audience.)*

NARRATOR: But, to this very day, Lucifer boasts:

VOICE of LUCIFER: Just because Jesus rose from the dead doesn't mean that I will stop trying to win!

(LUCIFER & SATANS laugh wildly from the shadows.)

VOICE of LUCIFER: "Someday, just you wait! I'LL GET YOU!"

(ANGEL MICHAEL, carrying Sword high, followed by ANGEL GABRIEL, ANGEL RAPHAEL & ANGELS laugh at LUCIFER & SATANS, who retreat further into the dark)

VOICE OF MICHAEL: Remain in Darkness, forever!

MUSICAL POSTLUDE   CURTAIN CALL.

The Crossmaker

A Parish Passion Play

by

Gerald Gurka, M .Div., M.Th., MA

CAST of CHARACTERS

NARRATOR 1.................. .... NARRATIONS, FEMALE VOICES
NARRATOR 2.................. .... ETHAN, MALE VOICES
NARRATOR 3........................FEMALE VOICES, NARRATIONS
NARRATOR 4........................MALE VOICES, NARRATIONS

(NOTE: These NARRATORS will read the narrations and play the various voices of the characters throughout the play.)

JESUS, ... youth/adult, the Son of God
MARY, ... Mother of Jesus
JOSEPH................................... Husband of Mary
ETHAN .... youth/adult, Childhood friend of Jesus/Crossmaker
JOHANNA................................ Mother of Ethan
CORNELIUS .... Assistant Centurion
LONGINIUS .... youth/adult—Head Centurion & Father of Lucas
LUCAS...................................... Young Guard, evil Son of Longinius
PONTIUS PILATE...................... Roman Procurator of Judea
CLAUDIA PROCLES .... Wife of Pontius Pilate
SIMON OF CYRENE .... African farmer, forced to help Jesus
CAIAPHAS .... Jerusalem High Priest/Enemy of Jesus
RABBI .... Celebrant at Mary & Joseph's wedding
ANN .... Mother of Mary
JOACHIM.................................. Father of Mary
ANNA the PROPHETESS.......... Devout Servant of God
SIMEON.................................... Prophet & Ancestor of Jesus
JOHN .... Beloved Disciple of Jesus

JUDAS .... Treasurer of Disciples & Traitor
PETER..................................... Head Disciple of Jesus
MARY MAGDALENE .... Galilean Woman cured by Jesus
VERONICA .... Used veil to wipe Jesus' face
MAIDSERVANT .... Young slave of Cornelius' household
JOANNA .... Secret Disciple of Jesus
TIRA.. Mother of Dismas & Lucas
GESTASs' MOTHER .... Jerusalem drunk & harlot
SAMARITAN WOMAN .... Outcast Woman helped by Jesus
WOMEN of JERUSALEM........... Vigilantes for Convicted Criminals
ARCHANGEL GABRIEL .... God's Primary Messenger
ARCHANGEL MICHAEL. .... God's Protector & Satan Adversary
ARCHANGEL RAPHAEL .... God's Healer
GUARDIAN ANGELS................ Mediators/Messengers of God
FATHER SATAN....................... Fallen Angel/Prince of Darkness
MOTHER SATAN...................... Wife of the Prince of Darkness
SON of SATAN .... Eager upstart Prince of Darkness
DAUGHTER of SATAN .... Conniving Princess of Darkness
GUARDS.................................. Assistants to the Centurions
BLIND YOUTH.......................... Cured by Jesus
WATER BOYS .... Young followers of Jesus
GESTAS .... Bad Thief crucified with Jesus
DISMAS .... Good Thief crucified with Jesus
JOHN THE BAPTIST .... Cousin/Forerunner of Jesus

CREW

CROSS DESIGN
LIGHTING DESIGN
SOUND DESIGN
MUSIC
HAIR & MAKEUP DESIGN
COSTUMES, PROPS, GREETERS & REFRESHMENTS

SETTINGS:
The Holy Land:
Nazareth, Bethlehem, Jordan River & Jerusalem during Passover
Week...from Palm Sunday to Easter Sunday

A NOTE from the AUTHOR:
Ideally, this play should be presented in a church building, making use
of the Main Sanctuary/altar and the center and Side aisles.
Lighting: Two follow-spot lights with color gels. Optional: Projections
and fog machine to highlight intense scenes. Additional Lighting may
be used.

Music: Pre-recorded music. Church Choir & Instrumentalists/or
combination thereof.

INTRODUCTION & LIGHTS UP

SCENE 1   ENGAGEMENT OF MARY AND JOSEPH

(MARY at center. JOSEPH at Church Entrance)

NARRATOR 1: In our hearts, birds sing when we meet the one we are
destined to truly love.

(LIGHTS UP. MARY enters, JOSEPH comes down aisle.)

NARRATOR 1: Joseph was an upright man, older than Mary. He may
have been a widower, with children from a previous marriage. The
name – Joseph – is an abbreviated form of the Hebrew Jehoseph"
...which means: "May Jahweh give an increase." *(JOSEPH kneels,
places ring on MARY'S finger.)* Engagements were considered as a true

marriage. *(MARY nods "yes". They embrace.)* However, not until the marriage ceremony, could the bride enter the house of her husband.

NARRATOR 1: God sent the angel Gabriel to a town in Galilee, named Nazareth. There, the angel made an announcement to Mary.

NARRATOR 4 *(as GABRIEL):* Peace Be with You! The Lord is with You, and has greatly Blessed You!

NARRATOR 1: Seeing Mary deeply troubled by His message, the Angel reassured Her.

NARRATOR 4 *(as GABRIEL)*: Don't be afraid, God has been gracious to You. You will become pregnant, and give birth to a son…and You will name Him, Jesus.

NARRATOR 3 *(as MARY):* I am a virgin how can this be?

SCENE 2   MARY AND HER PARENTS

(MARY is between ANNA(r) & JOACHIM (l) at center; JOSEPH & SATANS are right front; GABRIEL, MICHAEL, RAPHAEL, & ANGELS at left front)

NARRATOR 3 (as MARY): Yes, mother, I'm telling you the truth.   I said "yes" to the angel…I will accept this miracle – that my child, Jesus, will be born by the power of God's Holy Spirit.

(ANNA hugs MARY.)

NARRATOR 1: Anna believed her daughter, Mary…for she and her husband Joachim were desolate because of their childlessness.

(MARY & JOACHIM go to center. ANGEL GABRIEL joins MARY)

NARRATOR 1: One day, years ago, while Anna was praying, an angel appeared and told her that she would bear a child. In thanksgiving, Anna promised to dedicate this child to God.
(ANGEL RAPHAEL joins ANNA)

NARRATOR 1: On another occasion, Anna's husband, Joachim, *(ANGEL MICHAEL joins JOACHIM)* also had an angel visitor – promising a child.

(MARY joins ANNA, JOACHIM and ANGELS, at front. SATAN Family scoffs and moves toward them. Remaining ANGELS "angel flake" the Holy Family in protection. SATANS, angrily, back off. JOSEPH joins them and reaches out to MARY, then to parents)

NARRATOR 1: This Holy Family reminds all families to believe in their children...even when they want to protect them from making bad choices. Children deserve to be trusted until proven otherwise.

(SATANS approach & threaten ANGELS.)

SCENE THREE   THE MARRIAGE OF MARY AND JOSEPH

(MARY, JOSEPH, RABBI at entrance.   ANNA & JOACHIM at left.   SATANS at right and ANGELS at front.)

NARRATOR 4:   As we enter marriage, do we ever know what we are getting into?   Do we realize the commitment is for life? ...do we fully understand the vows we take and the toasts made on that day? *(RABBI gives glass; MARY and JOSEPH smash the glass.)* The joy and brokenness of the future which no one escapes.

NARRATOR 3:   Joseph wasn't bitter about Mary's pregnancy before marriage – he knew the child was not his own. When Mary told him the story he seriously thought of privately putting Mary away – without exposing her to shame. However, an Angel visit took care of that!
(ANGEL GABRIEL approaches JOSEPH and raises wings.)

NARRATOR 4 *(as GABRIEL)*: Joseph, do not be afraid. The child Mary carries is from God. He has a special mission and you are to call his name Jesus. Don't worry. I'll keep an eye on you two.

NARRATOR 3: In Bethlehem, during the census of the Emperor Augustus, Mary gave birth to Jesus, wrapped Him in swaddling clothes, and laid Him in a manger for there was no room for them to stay in the Inn.

(MARY, JOSEPH, BABY JESUS, front of altar. SATANS at right. MARY MAGDALENE & VERONICA AND WOMEN OF JERUSALEM with babies. ANNA & JOACHIM near MARY. ANGELS raise their wings. JOHANNA, and her baby at left. YOUNG LONGINIUS the CENTURION at aisle.)

SCENE 4   JESUS' BIRTH & THE HOLY INNOCENTS

NARRATOR 4: When King Herod learned that a baby king was born, he ordered all the boys around Bethlehem – under two years old--to be killed.

(As YOUNG LONGINIUS the CENTURION comes down aisle, the ANGELS protect MARY, JOSEPH and JOHANNA and their babies.)

NARRATOR 4: Many actions we choose in life take our innocence from us. We kill ourselves and our families with uncontrolled passions, jealousies, selfishness, envy…greed.

(LONGINIUS approaches MARY MAGDALENE and VERONICA, grabs their babies, throws them to the ground. LONGINIUS raises his sword to strike the first baby. ANGELS weep. SATANS laugh. Remaining WOMEN of JERUSALEM exit.)

NARRATOR 4: As the ruthless centurion took these innocent lives— their spilled blood splashed into his face and eyes.

(LONGINIUS wipes his face and eyes.)

NARRATOR 4: And, from that moment-- Longinius lost the light in his right eye. Because he was a soldier, he tried to hide his partial blindness. *(LONGINIUS kills second baby with sword.)* Perhaps, Mary Magdalene and Veronica lost their children in that blood fest, which continues today in the secret killing of the unborn.

A woman named Johanna visited the manger that night with her infant son, Ethan, *(JOHANNA, holding infant, enters.)* Mary & Joseph were spared from the order of the Slaughter of the Holy Innocents by the protection of angel wings. Johanna and Ethan became close friends to Jesus, Mary, and Joseph, Yet, friendships take their own detours. *(LONGINIUS looks sick. SATANS cheer LONGINIUS.)*

NARRATOR 4: *(LONGINIUS retches.)* Little did the Holy Family, Johanna, Ethan, Veronica and Mary Magdalene know they would meet this Centurion again, on a fateful Friday thirty-some years away.

NARRATOR 1: Many innocent families suffer unexplainable tragedy. Why do bad things happen to good people? We don't know, but we don't give up life. We can't stop loving our families or ourselves...because of the pain we experience if we are left here without them.

SCENE 5   THE PRESENTATION IN THE TEMPLE

(MARY, JOSEPH and BABY JESUS at center. ANNA the PROPHETESS at left. SIMEON at right.)

NARRATOR 1: As was the custom, on the eighth day, Mary and Joseph brought Jesus to the Temple to consecrate Him as the Law prescribed. *(JOSEPH raises BABY JESUS.)* They made the proper sacrifice in thanksgiving, with two turtle doves. *(MARY holds the two doves.)* Anna, a widow and prophetess, was present that day. *(ANNA the PROPHETESS goes to MARY.)*   So was Simeon. *(SIMEON goes to JOSEPH.)*

NARRATOR 4 *(as SIMEON):* I thank you, God, that you have allowed me to live to this day when I behold He who will be the downfall of many in Israel. Mother, your heart will be pierced, as with a sword. *(ANNA & SIMEON present BABY JESUS to the audience.)*

NARRATOR 1: This man and woman longed their whole lives to behold the Savior. They recognized the tiny Jesus as the fulfillment of the prophecies and accepted Him.

NARRATOR 3: Would we recognize the Savior? Will we invite Jesus to be part of our lives? After the Baptism of our children, how long before we acquaint them with God again?

SCENE 6   JOSEPH'S WORKSHOP

(Enter JOSEPH, guiding JESUS' hand with a saw, YOUNG ETHAN, holding a piece of wood beneath the saw)

NARRATOR 3: When the young family came back from Egypt, Joseph settled them in Nazareth, where he was a builder. Joseph's humble background as a carpenter would be a source of scandal to the critics of the adult Jesus. *(With love, JOSEPH'S hand guides JESUS' hand sawing the piece of wood.)* Joseph taught Jesus, and Ethan, his young friend the mastery of wood. *(ETHAN, smiling, holds upward the two cuts of wood.)* This young friend will use his woodworking talent to make crosses for the Roman Justice system, a fine paying position. Crucifixion was the means of executing criminals. Jesus, a better craftsman than Ethan, would grow up to author a New Covenant, illustrated by miracles and parables. *(JOSEPH embraces JESUS, then "high-5"s ETHAN.)*

MUSICAL INTERLUDE

(MARY sits center holding JOSEPH'S dead body. JESUS & ANGELS to MARY'S left. JOHANNA, holding ETHAN, to JESUS' left. SATANS, snickering, are at right.)
SCENE 7   JOSEPH'S   DEATH

NARRATOR 3: Jesus' beloved father, Joseph, died before the start of His public ministry. Joseph may have passed away, but his spirit lives on! Joseph lives on as the patron saint and protector of workingmen. He is also the patron saint of social justice and Fatherhood. When we lose our earthly fathers, we may wander into an empty desert with new temptations.

(SATANS tip-toe around ETHAN. ANGELS motion to leave. Mr. & Mrs. SATAN approach MARY and "play fiddle" in mockery. CHILD JESUS comforts MARY and pushes SATANS away. SATANS jeer at JESUS.)

NARRATOR 3: Regardless of our pain and loss, we pray to Jesus for strength and for St. Joseph's protection as we endure.

MUSICAL INTERLUDE

SCENE 8   JESUS' BAPTISM

(JOHN the BAPTIST and ADULT JESUS are between ANGELS (r & l).
JUDAS & SATANS are at right; JOHN the APOSTLE at left.)

NARRATOR 1: Jesus came from Galilee, to the Jordan River to be baptized by John. As John poured the water over Him, a light came down from Heaven. A voice like thunder spoke.

(JOHN the BAPTIST sprinkles water on JESUS' head.)

NARRATOR 2 *(as GOD):* This is my own dear Son, with Whom I am pleased.

(JOHN the BAPTIST and JOHN the APOSTLE embrace JESUS. JUDAS looks perplexed. SATANS circle JUDAS.)

NARRATOR 1: Many more were baptized that day. This was the institution of Baptism as the ritual to become a follower of Jesus. Today, we bring our children to church for Baptism. Why? Some wrongly, we see Baptism as a kind of spiritual vaccination to safeguard our children until the time of their First Communion. But, more accurately, Baptism is the formal initiation into the family of God. It is a symbol of eternal relationship with God, and with our earthly family. Loving families keep in touch, and visit regularly.

(JESUS & MARY enter with JOHN the APOSTLE (r) and MARY MAGDALENE (l). JUDAS stands near JOHN the APOSTLE. Remaining CAST is holding palms, raised high; SATANS & CAIAPHAS at front; BLIND CHILD, with a bandage- wrapped eyes at center.)

SCENE 9   PALM SUNDAY

NARRATOR 2:   Three years later, Palm Sunday is a glorious day for Jesus and His family of disciples.   Hailed as a King in the streets of Jerusalem, Jesus again causes jealousy in the ruling class. As with all days of glory, not everyone is happy for our success.

NARRATORS AND CAST: Hosanna, Hosanna!

(CAIAPHAS & SATANS look jealous and begin blaming each other.)

NARRATOR 1: A Blind Child was in the crowd, pressing closer to the King.   *(BLIND CHILD makes his way to Jesus.)*

NARRATOR 2: He could see Jesus through his sense of touch.

(JESUS stoops down and BLIND CHILD touches His face. JESUS removes the bandages and touches the CHILD'S eyes...they embrace.)

NARRATOR 2: As we mature, do we identify with the people in the streets, shouting for the newest King, only to turn our backs on Him the next day; or are we the establishment, jealous and critical of anyone who offers new ideas?   Jesus asks us to live simply, help our neighbor, and trust God as a child trusts his parents. Are we afraid that a miracle will happen? A miracle that calls for a change in us.

NARRATORS AND CAST: Hosanna, Hosanna!

(ENTIRE CAST, holding palms, dances around JESUS. CAIAPHAS hands JUDAS a palm. JUDAS throws it to the ground.)

NARRATOR 2: *(as palm hits ground.)* Some of us think we should be getting all the attention...

(SATANS & CAIAPHAS "cuddle" JUDAS.)

NARRATOR 1: ...as Judas felt on Palm Sunday.

(SATANS & CAIAPHAS offer JUDAS coins. A greedy JUDAS opens his palms to receive money. CAIAPHAS drops the coins into JUDAS' palms; SATANS intercept the money. JUDAS tries to retrieve the coins.

NARRATOR 4 *(as CAIAPHAS):* Now, now, let's not be greedy!

NARRATOR 1: Jealousy is called a "deadly" sin for good reason. Success of a friend or family member can drive a self-centered person to unimaginable activities. Then come the associates of Jealousy: Envy and Greed. They make deadly friends.

(JUDAS gets coins and exits with CAIAPHAS—as if team mates. SATANS follow with "loser" sign.)

MUSIC INTERLUDE

SCENE 10   THE LAST SUPPER

(JESUS, with towel on shoulder, holds water pitcher & bowl. JUDAS is in front of altar. MARY, MARY MAGDALENE, JOHANNA, ADULT ETHAN, VERONICA, CHILDREN, APOSTLES gather around altar. ANGELS stand at center; SATANS right front. altar is set with cloth, lit candles, cup, and dish holding bread.)

NARRATOR 3: Celebrations with family and friends, whether birthdays, anniversaries, graduations, or holidays involve a sumptuous meal. The food is more special because it is shared with others, not because of what is served. Being present, together, is more important than the meal. As years go by and loved ones pass away or move away, these celebrations become memories as well. In effect, our family tables become sacred places.

(JESUS washes then dries JUDAS' feet.)

NARRATOR 3: At family tables, altars, and wherever meals are celebrated, love is a main ingredient.

(JESUS & JUDAS walk to their places at the altar. ANGELS reach towards JESUS. CAST, perplexed, look at each other. SATANS mock.)

NARRATOR 3: Jesus took the bread, said the Blessing, broke it, and gave it to them.

NARRATOR 4 *(as JESUS):* Take it. This is My Body.

(JESUS raises the bread for all to see.)

NARRATOR 3: Then Jesus took a cup and gave thanks.

NARRATOR 4 *(as JESUS):* This is the blood of the new covenant that will be shed for many. Do this in memory of Me.

(JESUS raises the cup. JUDAS looks bored. BOY SATAN shoves JUDAS in the back.)

NARRATOR 3: Sadly, at these special meals, resentment, discontent, and unresolved issues often raise their ugly heads.
(JUDAS pushes JOHN away. JUDAS exits with JESUS watching.)

NARRATOR 3: Judas was disappointed in Jesus. How often do these betrayals happen in families? Judas wanted a political Messiah, not a spiritual one. Parents wish their children could be everything the parent never became. Children want their parents to bail them out of every mess, and harbor resentment when parents have had enough.

(JUDAS walks away from JESUS and then looks back. BOY SATAN pushes JUDAS as other SATANS join JUDAS. JESUS watches, troubled. MARY & CAST comfort JESUS.)

NARRATOR 3: Often family and friends confuse expectations with results. They are unwilling to praise success, because of what their expectations dictate.

SCENE 11   GARDEN

(JESUS & JOHN the APOSTLE in front of altar; ANGELS at left.)

NARRATOR 1: Evil pushes us into wrong gardens of behavior. We allow seeds of hate to bloom. We prune the rose buds instead of the thorns. At Gethsemane was an Olive Garden where Jesus regularly taught His family of disciples to pray. What seeds do we plant in the gardens of our lives? Seeds of love...trust...forgiveness? Or seeds of hate and betrayal?

(ANGELS approach JOHN the APOSTLE & JESUS as they are praying.)

NARRATOR 1: Jesus loved coming to this Garden to spend alone time, in prayer, with God, His Father.

(As JESUS kneels in prayer, JOHN the APOSTLE yawns and falls asleep.)

NARRATOR 1: True prayer never desires control of another person.

(SATANS enter and mock JESUS' prayer. JUDAS, LONGINIUS, the HEAD CENTURION, CORNELIUS the ASSISTANT CENTURION, GUARDS & LUCAS enter.)

NARRATOR 1: True prayer helps us want what is best for others, as well as for us. True prayer seeks strength and understanding; courage to face issues we can't control.

(SATANS tip toe to front, and give "loser" sign to JESUS. ANGELS raise wings protecting JOHN & JESUS. CAIAPHAS enters, greets the SATANS with a "High-5." SATANS whistle. JUDAS leads CENTURIONS & GUARDS down center. CAIAPHAS & SATANS retreat. JESUS remains deep in prayer. GUARDS push JUDAS towards JESUS; SATANS shove JUDAS into JESUS. JUDAS betrays JESUS with a "kiss." LUCAS wakes JOHN the APOSTLE. JOHN breaks free; LONGINIUS & CORNELIUS shove JESUS to ground. ANGELS weep. CAIAPHAS rubs his hands in glee. SATANS stamp pitchforks on the floor.)

NARRATOR 4:   Some people rejoice in others' misfortune. It's difficult to believe that even family, who should love us, betray us. Jesus, our Brother, experienced this horror on Holy Thursday Night.

SCENE 12   TRIAL, SCOURGING, CROSS

PONTIUS PILATE & CLAUDIA, PILATE'S WIFE are at center; MARY, MARY MAGDALENE, and JOHN the APOSTLE in front of altar; JOHANNA, VERONICA, WOMEN of JERUSALEM at left; ANGELS and SATANS, JUDAS, CAIAPHAS at right and left center. JESUS, hands are tied. LONGINIUS the HEAD CENTURION, CORNELIUS the ASSISTANT CENTURION, GUARDS, and ETHAN the CROSSMAKER, holding a huge cross, are in the back. LUCAS & GUARDS hold whips, cloak & Crown of Thorns at front.)

NARRATOR 4: Pontius Pilate was a self-absorbed ruler and husband. His wife was a better leader than he. They lived in Herod, the madman's house, he who was responsible for the murder of Holy Innocents at the time of Jesus' Birth. Pilate, by his lack of action and his failure to be responsible, will permit the murder of another Holy Innocent.

(LONGINIUS & CORNELIUS push JESUS down. They stop MARY from comforting JESUS.)

NARRATOR 4:   As parents, are we afraid to use our authority? Pilate didn't use his authority to stop the travesty of Jesus' trial and sentence.

(CENTURIONS shove JESUS in front of PONTIUS PILATE)

NARRATOR 4:   Or, do we avoid making responsible decisions, by failing to address the real issue? This only causes needless pain.

NARRATOR 2 (*as PONTIUS PILATE):* Take Him away. I wash my hands of this Man.

(PILATE gestures to have JESUS removed. CLAUDIA becomes angry. LONGINIUS & CORNELIUS push JESUS to front. LUCAS & GUARDS bring whips, red cloak and Crown of Thorns. CORNELIUS strips JESUS. LONGINIUS signals, then GUARDS whip JESUS. LONGINIUS places the Crown of Thorns on JESUS head. JESUS bows His head; GUARDS dress JESUS in red cloak. SATANS, with palm branches, circle JESUS, mocking. SATANS hand palm branches to GUARDS who strike JESUS over the head. LUCAS & GUARDS place palm branches in JESUS' arms. ANGELS & CAST sorrowfully react.)

NARRATOR 4: *(LUCAS hysterically laughs.)* Let's not forget the times we allow popular opinion to influence our judgment of right or wrong. Yes, popular opinion – the flavor of the month.

(GUARDS force JESUS to his feet, center)
NARRATOR 4: The popular flavor often isn't right or just. Pontius Pilate knew that and so did Claudia, his wife. Loving spouses instinctively see and tell what is right for their loved one. Pontius Pilate should have listened to his wife that Good Friday. Husbands, Wives, be open, listen to each other. Be willing to face the truth.

(LONGINIUS the HEAD CENTURION goes to center pointing at ETHAN the CROSSMAKER.)

SCENE 13   ETHAN THE CROSSMAKER

NARRATOR 1: Thirty years ago, Longinius started his military career with the slaughter of the Holy Innocents. Angels protected Mary, Joseph, and the Infant Jesus from him. He also overlooked Johanna and her infant, Ethan, who were visiting the manger that night. Miraculously, their lives were spared.

(LUCAS walks behind LONGINIUS, slapping him on the back like a winning team-mate.)

NARRATOR 1: Now, with his son, Lucas, an image of his father in cruelty as well as looks, Longinius will commit another atrocious crime.

(LONGINIUS helps ETHAN carry the Cross. LUCAS, snickering, follows. ETHAN is horrified as he recognizes JESUS.)

NARRATOR 2 (*as ETHAN*): No! Jesus! Is this you? My friend! We were boys when your Father, Joseph, taught us the art of woodworking.

(*ETHAN drops the cross. JOHANNA rushes to help him, then looks at MARY with sorrow.*)

NARRATOR 2 (*as ETHAN*): Mother, help me. I have made the instrument of death for my friend.

(*LONGINIUS and CORNELIUS jam the cross onto JESUS' shoulders.*)

 NARRATOR 2 (*As ETHAN*): Jesus, please forgive me. I didn't know this would happen. I thought it was such a good job. I never thought about who might be hurt by my actions.

(*JOHANNA begins to cry.*)

NARRATOR 1: Sometimes, we are all victims of circumstance.

(*ETHAN is stricken as JOHANNA asks JESUS for forgiveness. CAIAPHAS gloats.*)

 NARRATOR 1: Mary Magdalene and Veronica lost their babies that terrible night thirty-three years ago. They wonder that Ethan's life was spared for this.

(*JOHN the APOSTLE to MARY MAGDALENE & VERONICA, trying to calm them. JUDAS looks at CAIAPHAS*)

NARRATOR 4 (*as JUDAS*): I betrayed Jesus worse than his childhood friend. Ethan never imagined someone he knew would hang on a cross. I sold Jesus to the authorities for thirty pieces of silver. I knew what I was doing.

(LONGINIUS & CORNELIUS push JESUS, carrying cross, to front. As JESUS passes JUDAS, he looks directly at him. JUDAS stares back.)

SCENE 14   JUDAS' DEATH

(JUDAS, holding a pouch containing silver coins, approaches CAIAPHAS. SATANS at left front MR. SATAN holds a noose.)

NARRATOR 3:   If we welcome evil into our lives, we need to be prepared for the consequences.

(JUDAS throws money at CAIAPHAS who laughs and exits.   SATANS tip-toe to JUDAS.   MR. SATAN hands JUDAS the noose.)

NARRATOR 3:   Evil has no boundaries; evil even gets rid of evil to achieve its goals. *(JUDAS to center with the noose.)*

NARRATOR 4 *(as JUDAS):*   Who can take this death from me? Who forgives? I am lost.

NARRATOR 3:   Which of us is a Judas? As a brother, sister, son, daughter, mother, father, husband, wife, do we have demons? Have we made grave mistakes and mistakenly believe we are doomed? Do our demons obscure forgiveness? We know who forgives. It is Jesus. *(SATANS encourage JUDAS.)*

NARRATOR 4 *(as JUDAS):*   I deserve to die. Even as a child, I made my father so angry that he hit me and my mother too. It was all my fault. Then, I was hitting my brothers and sisters and others too. I'm no good. The world is better off without me.

NARRATOR 3: Judas' vision was so dark, he couldn't let the light of forgiveness, the Light of Christ transform his pain.

(Frightened, JUDAS runs out, holding up the noose)

NARRATOR 3: In today's world, we tailor-fit our own nooses. It happens when we fail to bring our pain, our darkness to God. It's deadly when we refuse to forgive ourselves and one another.

SCENE 15   PILATE'S DEMISE

(PONTIUS PILATE & his wife, CLAUDIA, enter.)

NARRATOR 1 (as CLAUDIA): Evil actions create their own domino effect. I have a husband, Pontius Pilate, but I have always been alone. He is obsessed with work, then spends time with other women. If I try to talk about it, he gets angry and calls himself a failure. I would love him if he would let me.

(PONTIUS PILATE waves at CLAUDIA in disgust)

NARRATORS AND CAST: Give us Barabbas! Crucify Jesus! Crucify him.

NARRATOR 4 (as PILATE): Now the people are chanting for me to send Jesus to death. I know it is out of jealousy that He was arrested and charged. (MR. SATAN hands PONTIUS PILATE a noose.) My wife, Claudia told me not to pass judgment on Jesus. If this goes wrong, I fail as a procurator, fail as a husband, fail as a man. Everyone will be better off when I'm gone.

(SATANS enter applauding.)

NARRATOR 1 *(as CLAUDIA):* He couldn't see his faults. He wouldn't admit making poor choices. So often, I tried to advise him. Recently, it was about Jesus. I sent word to him of my dream about Jesus, and told Pontius not to involve himself in the case. If only he admitted his mistakes, and owned up to his failures, we could get our lives back on track. But, now, who knows what will happen?

(PONTIUS PILATE exits with the noose)

SCENE 16   THE GOOD & BAD THIEVES

(DISMAS, the Good Thief, and GESTAS, the Bad Thief, with their crosses, ANGELS, WOMEN, GUARD, SATANS, CAIAPHAS at right and left front)

NARRATOR 3   On Good Friday, Two Thieves were crucified with Jesus. What fate brought them to that door? We might wonder what their family lives were like. Were they raised in good homes or in the streets?

(DISMAS at left & GESTAS at right.)

NARRATOR 2: Even the best of families have members that turn out both well and badly. Were these two thieves, Dismas and Gestas, *(DISMAS & GESTAS, carrying crosses, go to center)* like the Prodigal Son and his brother? The younger one takes his Father's money, leaves home, and squanders everything. The older brother freely chooses to be jealous and resentful of his father's generosity to his younger brother. The older brother might be like Gestas, the Bad Thief. *(GESTAS snarls at cast and audience)*

NARRATOR 3: Gestas resents everyone and everything. He refuses to see any goodness in others and is jealous of anyone he thinks gets ahead of him.

(CAIAPHAS enters, laughs at GESTAS, who glares at CAIAPHAS, who sticks his tongue out at GESTAS.).

NARRATOR 3:   Even as he is nailed to a cross, Gestas curses everyone. He mocks Jesus, demanding that Jesus perform a miracle. If the legend is true, Gestas' eyes were plucked out by a crow while he hung on the cross. A perfect symbol for our blindness to our own weakness. *(GESTAS beats his chest.)* Gestas couldn't believe in the possibility of transformation.   He was trapped in the Evil of selfishness.

(GUARDS raise GESTAS on his cross. GUARDS, CAIAPHAS and SATANS laugh at him.)

NARRATOR 2:   How can we imagine Dismas?   Maybe he met the Infant Jesus in the manger, that first Christmas Night.

(DISMAS is nailed and roped to his cross. He remains silent, head bowed. ANGELS, empathizing, open their wings. GESTAS mocks DISMAS & SATANS signal "Loser".)

NARRATOR 2: Dismas was an unwanted child. He had no one in his life to show him good, yet he desired to be good. He lived in the stable where Joseph and Mary came for the birth of Jesus. Dismas saw three Wise Men come to a stable and place gifts of gold, frankincense, and myrrh before the tiny Baby born there. His generous heart wanted to give a gift also. All he had was his drum. So he gave the gift of music. Now, on Good Friday, Dismas… the Drummer Boy…the welcomed- home Prodigal Son, encounters Jesus again.

(DISMAS looks longingly at Jesus)

NARRATOR 4 *(as DISMAS):* Shut up, Gestas! We deserve to be on our cross today, but this man has done nothing wrong.

NARRATOR 2: In spite of his years without love and his criminal activities, Dismas reaches out to Jesus. This time he makes a request.

NARRATOR 4 *(as DISMAS)* Jesus, I deserve to die here for my crimes, but, will you please remember me when you come into your Kingdom?

NARRATOR 2 *(as JESUS)* Dismas, I remember you, and I promise you that this day, you will be with me in paradise.

(DISMAS face is filled with joy)

NARRATOR 3: We see how like the prodigal son is our imagined Dismas. Our joy comes from knowing that we also have Jesus' promise to be united with the love and forgiveness of God the Father. *(ANGELS reach toward DISMAS.)*

SCENE 17   JESUS BEARS HIS CROSS / FALLS

(JESUS is bearing Cross; LONGINIUS, CORNELIUS, LUCAS at center; Two WATER BOYS at front)

NARRATOR 1: As Jesus' hands embrace the Cross, he recalls years of handling wood in Joseph's carpentry shop. There he shaped raw wood into beautiful furniture. Now, the carpenter's Son from Nazareth transforms a wooden instrument of death into the symbol of salvation for all people. His Mother, Mary, looks on in sadness.

(Two WATER BOYS offer JESUS water. LUCAS knocks the water from their hands. LONGINIUS scares the WATER BOYS away. LUCAS strikes JESUS, knocking Him to the ground, with cross falling onto His back.

CORNELIUS *stares at LUCAS. LONGINIUS tries to stop LUCAS from kicking JESUS.)*

NARRATOR 3 *(as MARY)*: That cross must be heavy. It stands for the sins of all mankind. My precious Son is beaten, exhausted, but not defeated. Isn't that crossmaker Ethan? Johanna's son, who grew up with Jesus, apprentice to my husband, Joseph? This will be tragic for them.

(JOHN the APOSTLE, MARY, MARY MAGDALENE, & ANGELS run to help JESUS. LUCAS pushes JOHN away. MARY and MARY MAGDALENE comfort JESUS.)

 NARRATOR 3 *(as MARY)*: Be strong, My Son. You are the light of my life and the light of the world. An unexpected friend is here. It is Ethan and his mother, Johanna.

(ETHAN the CROSSMAKER, and his mother, JOHANNA comfort MARY.)

NARRATOR 1:   The Crossmaker and his mother are devastated to find Jesus, Ethan's childhood friend carrying a cross to his death. How many parents are ashamed of the occupations of their children?

(JOHANNA and ETHAN look beseechingly at MARY, as if she can explain this monstrous circumstance.)

NARRATOR 3 *(as MARY)*: Johanna, your heart breaks like mine for our sons. Both doing what they were born to do, and now looking into the depths of fear. Mothers know the hearts of their children.

(ETHAN goes to help JESUS. SATANS and GUARDS point & laugh at ETHAN. LUCAS pushes ETHAN, who falls next to JESUS. GUARDS force JESUS & ETHAN to their feet.   LUCAS strikes ETHAN, JOHANNA runs to

help but GUARDS shove her away. LONGINIUS &   CORNELIUS place cross on JESUS' shoulders. MARY goes to help JOHANNA.)

NARRATOR 1:   Yet, as parents must, Mary had the courage to intervene in her Son's unjust punishment.

(LUCAS pushes ETHAN and JOHANNA back.   MARY   places her hands atop JESUS' hands and walks with Him. ANGELS bow to MARY & JESUS. GUARDS, GESTAS, SATANS mock.)

NARRATOR 1:   We often run from others' pain or injury. We think we have better things to do.   Or, just the opposite, we stay in hurtful situations when we should leave. Mary walked every step with her Son. She didn't want this for Him, but she was there a rock of support.

(MARY & JESUS walk to center. GUARDS ready to strike MARY.   ETHAN comes forward to protect MARY but is held back by LUCAS. JOHN & MARY MAGDALENE help MARY move back. JOHANNA approaches JESUS.)

NARRATOR 1:   We need not apologize for the actions of our adult children. They will rise or fall by themselves. We always love them, even when we do not love their actions.   Johanna wanted to apologize to Jesus and Mary for Ethan building the cross. But an apology was not necessary. Jesus looked deeply into her eyes and Johanna knew that Jesus drew strength from Ethan's cross.

(CAIAPHAS, SATANS, GESTAS mock JOHANNA.   GUARDS push JESUS who falls to ground with cross falling beside him. MARY runs back to JESUS but is held back by JOHN & MARY MAGDALENE. MARY's hands reach to JESUS.)

NARRATOR 1:   Yes, in the midst of overwhelming terror on Good Friday, Jesus' friends and family felt a powerful, transcendent love.

Even though they were powerless to help, they were comforted by Jesus.

(JOHN the APOSTLE & MARY MAGDALENE escort MARY as they follow the cross).

SCENE 18   SIMON OF CYRENE

(Enter SIMON of CYRENE, with a basket of eggs, and   CORNELIUS, scouting the audience)

NARRATOR 3:   Family members often pull us into unwelcome situations; like Simon of Cyrene who was chosen to help Jesus carry His Cross.

(GUARDS run into SIMON who drops his basket, LUCAS juggles the eggs)

NARRATOR 4 (as SIMON):   Hey, what are you doing? Those eggs are for my customers! What? Why me? I don't know you. Wait! Is that the Man they call Jesus? What's he done? Of course I'll help Jesus. Anything I can do.

(CORNELIUS AND LUCAS push SIMON away, then LONGINIUS & GUARDS raise JESUS up and drop the cross on His shoulders. JESUS nearly collapses. LONGINIUS orders SIMON to carry JESUS' cross)

NARRATOR 3: Sometimes, God answers our prayers through the help of others. Sometimes, we have to let go of our crosses as Jesus did. Mysteriously, God answers our prayers by forcing us to face the things we want to let go of.

(LONGINIUS shoves JESUS forward. CORNELIUS directs SIMON to follow. CAIAPHAS "air-fiddles." CAST reacts.)

SCENE 19 VERONICA

(VERONICA enters and stops, shocked at the sight of Jesus)

NARRATOR 2: Veronica remembers the day Jesus healed her bleeding. She was one of the tragic mothers who lost their infant the night the Holy Innocents were murdered. Now, Veronica can say thank you for her healing.

(As VERONICA goes to JESUS, MR. SATAN in mock sympathy throws rose petals on VERONICA as she passes him. ANGELS bow to VERONICA.)

NARRATOR 2:   A person who has suffered great loss might be afraid to help another sufferer. Yet helping someone else can release such feelings. Like Veronica, step in and become human angels to each other.

(JOHANNA and ETHAN enter in time to see VERONICA remove her veil & wipe JESUS' face. CAIAPHAS mocks VERONICA'S actions.   SATANS pretend to "choke."   LONGINIUS prods VERONICA back with his spear.)

NARRATOR 4: Ties of loving gratitude can be thicker than ties of blood.
(As VERONICA gently pulls her veil back from JESUS, SATANS gleefully pull at the veil and push her. VERONICA falls face down into her veil. As she rises, she is unaware that the imprint of JESUS' face is on the veil facing the audience. VERONICA exits.)

SCENE 20   WOMEN OF JERUSALEM

(Enter two WOMEN, holding babies, and TWO CHILDREN to center. MOTHER of the GOOD THIEF, TIRA, JOHANNA, ETHAN the CROSSMAKER at left front, MOTHER of BAD THIEF at right front)

NARRATOR 1:   Some of the Women of Jerusalem were Mothers of the Holy Innocents.   They endured the shocking loss of a child, but they trusted God and were open to future Blessings.

(WOMAN holding baby walks down center aisle)

NARRATOR 1: Yes, second chances—like the time Jesus met this Samaritan Woman at Jacob's Well.

(WOMAN approaches JESUS.   GESTAS sneers at WOMAN as she walks to JESUS; WOMAN ignores GESTAS.   SATANS gesture a "thumbs-up" to the WOMAN.)

NARRATOR 1:   Although this woman had more than one failed marriage, Jesus knew she needed to be understood, forgiven, and valued…the Blessings of True Love.

(TIRA, MOTHER of the GOOD THIEF, enters, SIMON of CYRENE removes cross from JESUS' shoulder)

NARRATOR 1: Some children grow up to be disappointments to their parents.

(MOTHER of GOOD THIEF scolds DISMAS; SATANS mock her.)

NARRATOR 1: Some parents become disappointments to their children. Dismas' mother was an absentee parent. Hearing that Dismas was in Jerusalem that day, she brings her pain to foot of the crosses.

(MOTHER of the BAD THIEF enters.)

NARRATOR 2:   Every child and parent can achieve their dreams. They can put their energies to good, or waste their lives in evil choices.

NARRATOR 3 *(as GESTAS' MOTHER)*: So, this is what you meant when you said your career is on the rise! So, where is the money hidden? C'mon, you can tell your old mother.

NARRATOR 2:   Children often follow a path similar to their parents. This can be true of good or bad paths.

(GESTAS sneers at his mother.)

NARRATOR 2: Gestas' Mother introduced him to a life of crime at an early age...small items--an apple--or grape at market. Larger items as he grew older. Once, she sold him into slavery for a bottle. When she heard he was in town, why not one last shake-down? Children return the love, respect--or lack of love, lack of respect-- that they are shown.

(SATANS tease GESTAS' MOTHER)

NARRATOR 4:   Yet, it is a mistake for parents to think it is too late for their children, or for themselves, to improve.

(2nd WOMAN, holding baby, & TWO CHILDREN walk down center.)

NARRATOR 4: For a moment, the lives of these women and their children, meet ultimate Goodness, ultimate Love in Jesus.

(ANGELS bow to 2nd WOMAN & TWO CHILDREN. SATANS try to stop WOMAN from reaching JESUS. CORNELIUS, LUCAS & GUARDS try to pull the WOMAN away from JESUS.).)

NARRATOR 4:   The Roman Guards had no respect for women or children. Some families don't respect each other, parents staying on the sidelines, children ignoring their parents.

(ETHAN the CROSSMAKER, looking perplexed, enters, looks around for JOHANNA, his mother.)

NARRATOR 3 *(as JOHANNA):* Oh, Ethan, I wish I could have protected you from this terrible day. If only I had been more loving, paid more attention to you, advised you not to work for the Romans.

NARRATOR 4: Life can be full of blessings or full of regrets. Like Johanna, once we get from God what we want, we forget about what God wants from us, until a day like today.

(JESUS reaches out to TIRA, GESTAS' MOTHER, JOHANNA, and the other women.)

NARRATOR 4:   Jesus touched the hearts and souls of these women. His actions empower us to reach and touch others, even if we don't know them.

(GUARDS jab DISMAS & GESTAS with sticks. LONGINIUS orders SIMON of CYRENE & JESUS to pick up the cross.)

SCENE 21   JESUS' GREAT FALL

NARRATOR 3: *(As SIMON of CYRENE & JESUS place the cross upon their shoulders)* Yes, at times, even the best of families can be like a rose, beautiful blooms, and painful thorns. *(JESUS & SIMON of CYRENE, slowly carry the heavy cross. LUCAS strikes SIMON & JESUS; JESUS collapses—in spectacular fashion—with cross catapulting to the floor.)*

NARRATOR 3: *(As Cross lands)* Family, friends and co-workers sometimes delight when relatives, siblings, the ex-wife, the ex-husband, favored son or daughter   crash and burn, especially from a tall pedestal.

(SIMON of CYRENE, enraged, fights with GUARDS. ANGELS & SATANS draw near.)

NARRATOR 3: A fall from grace, from the seemingly perfect marriage, from the apparently wonder job, a foreclosure, repossession of a car, a filing for   bankruptcy,   a loss of dignity, popularity or fame, spiral us into an uncertain place.

(SIMON of CYRENE tries to assist JESUS, but the SATANS grab SIMON'S left arm while the ANGELS   grab SIMON'S right arm—as if he were in the middle of a tug-of-war.)

SCENE 22   STRIPPING OF JESUS' GARMENTS

(JESUS' Cross is centered on the floor between the crosses of DISMAS & GESTAS; JESUS, LONGINIUS, CORNELIUS, LUCAS, with dice, at center; ANGELS at left front MARY, MARY MAGDALENE, VERONICA & JOHN the APOSTLE are at foot of JESUS' Cross. SIMON of CYRENE stands right & JOHANNA, ETHAN, left.

NARRATOR 1:   There are good strippings…and there are bad strippings in our lives. The Good Thief, Dismas, though stripped of his clothes and his dignity that day, became a Disciple of Jesus.

(GUARD tears off DISMAS' garments & then begins to rope DISMAS to the cross.)

NARRATOR 4 *(as DISMAS)*: Master, we deserve our fate today on the cross, but you have done nothing wrong. Please remember me when you come into your Kingdom.

NARRATOR 1: Dismas desired to clothe himself with the prayer of trust...the trust that he would have a share in Jesus' Heavenly Kingdom, unlike Judas whose sole interest was in an Earthly Kingdom. Dismas is the patron saint for families who face a death sentence.

(DISMAS looks prayerfully upward.   GUARD snickers.)

NARRATOR 1: The Bad Thief, Gestas, continued to strip himself of any goodness. Mocking Jesus and demanding a miracle.

NARRATOR 2 *(as GESTAS);* Hey, Miracle Man! You saved others, how about saving yourself and me too!

NARRATOR 1· As Jesus was strippod of Hio garment, the guards and soldiers threw dice to see who would get to keep the seamless robe Mary made him.

(LUCAS wins, raising/swirling garment in victory!)

NARRATOR 1: Jesus might have been talking about his own trial when he said "Blessed are you when they insult you, and persecute you, and utter every kind of evil falsely, against you, because of me."

(CORNELIUS throws JESUS to the ground. MARY reaches out to JESUS. LONGINIUS, CORNELIUS & LUCAS stretch JESUS' body on the cross. LUCAS, laughing, flaunts JESUS' garment & dice at MARY.)

NARRATOR 1:   Unfortunately, good people allow themselves to become corrupted. They give in to shameful values, practices, and habits. *(LONGINIUS at JESUS' left; CORNELIUS at JESUS' right; LUCAS at JESUS' feet; they raise hammers high.)*

SCENE 23 NAILING

(CAIAPHAS & SATAN FAMILY hold up nails as if the nails were the Statue of Liberty torch. ANGELS, MARY, MARY MAGDALENE, JOHN the APOSTLE, & VERONICA are at left of Cross. CAIAPHAS, impatient, grabs nails from SATANS and distributes to LONGINIUS, CORNELIUS & LUCAS place nails into JESUS' hands and feet...then raise their hammers high. ETHAN runs forward.)

NARRATOR 2 *(as ETHAN):* You only crucified criminals on my crosses before! WHY do you use nails today, and on this innocent Man?

(CAIAPHAS belly-laughs and snorts like a pig.)

NARRATOR 3: Lucas only wanted to get the job done, to go home, and celebrate the Roman Saturnalia. With time, Lucas became desensitized to killing.

(LUCAS shoves ETHAN raises his hammer & strikes ETHAN on side of head. ETHAN falls to the ground. JOHANNA and MARY rush to ETHAN)

NARRATOR 3: Despite Mary's own pain, she reaches out to help, to heal....

(ETHAN sits up. JOHANNA embraces ETHAN. JOHN the APOSTLE embraces MARY.)

NARRATOR 3: Never underestimate the intercession of a loving Mother. Many miracles, not recorded in Scripture, came from Mary's love that day. There is a prayer called "The Silent Prayer of Nailing."

If we are in a situation beyond our control, simply open the palms of our hands welcoming whatever is about to happen...and trust in God's providential care.

(SOUND EFFECTS: Hammering/Nailing (LONGINIUS, CORNELIUS, LUCAS nail JESUS to Cross. JESUS writhes in violent pain. MARY nears fainting, CAIAPHAS, laughing, pushes MARY back. JOHN the APOSTLE & MARY MAGDALENE assist MARY. CAIAPHAS hands Sign to LONGINIUS.)

NARRATOR 3:   The sign placed, on Jesus' Cross, mocked Jesus with the title: "He Claimed to Be King of the Jews."

(MRS. SATAN mocks MARY'S tears.)

NARRATOR: What mocking do we hammer into family or friends?

(Cross set in stand at center. JESUS stands crucified on Cross/ ANGELS stand behind cross, with MARY, MARY MAGDALENE AND JOHN in front of the cross. Nearby are JOHANNA & ETHAN. WOMEN of JERUSALEM, CHILDREN, CAST are kneeling in front of altar; they are grieving: some, refusing to look, have their heads buried in their hands...or turned away.)

(SOUND EFFECTS: THUNDER   LIGHTNING   CREEPY LAUGHTER)

NARRATOR 3:   The true test of the Cross...of the Crosses we all carry ...is the painful process of saying the unexpected, yet sometimes necessary, goodbyes. But, is it really goodbye? Or is it a welcoming?

SCENE 24 CRUCIFIXION

(JESUS, looking upward, breathes heavily. His body writhes. SOUND EFFECTS: (Throughout scene) THUNDER   LIGHTNING

NARRATOR 4 (as JESUS): Forgive them Father...for they don't know what they are doing. *(Long Pause)* I thirst.

(LONGINIUS, placing sponge on tip of spear, raises it to JESUS' lips. JESUS refuses)

NARRATOR 4 *(as JESUS)*: My God, My God! Why? Have You abandoned Me?

(LONGINIUS readies spear to kill JESUS. JOHANNA approaches.)

NARRATOR 1: Johanna thought there was something familiar about the older Centurion. Yes, she definitely recognized him.

(JOHANNA abruptly grabs LONGINIUS' spear)

NARRATOR 3 *(as JOHANNA)*: You're the One! Thirty-some years ago, I met you in Bethlehem at your Inn. You may not remember – but, you spared Jesus' life--He was that Infant born in the manger. I was there, too – with my Infant son, Ethan, your Crossmaker! The Angels protected us! You gave all of us safe haven. You can't take Jesus' life today! Please!! Please!!

(JOHANNA falls on her knees)

NARRATOR 4 *(as JESUS)*: Father, It is Finished. Into Your Hands, I place my Spirit.

(LONGINIUS raises spear...pauses...looks down at JOHANNA...then looks at JESUS...then, again, at JOHANNA. LONGINIUS hands his spear to LUCAS.)

NARRATOR: Some of us are propelled into the horrible choice of maintaining life ...or ending it.

(LUCAS, steps back, readies spear to pierce JESUS.)

NARRATOR 3 *(as JOHANNA):* NO!

NARRATOR 1: Unfairly, life forces us to make decisions where no one wins.
.
(LUCAS hands the spear back to LONGINIUS.)
NARRATOR 1: Like Lucas, we have to give up, give back. Yet, our jobs, our families, our friends demand situations where we should not go.

(LONGINIUS steps center & waves his spear. Then, like a knight in a jousting tournament, LONGINIUS charges and plunges spear into JESUS. MARY rushes to kiss JESUS' feet. LONGINIUS drops Spear. LUCAS removes the nails from JESUS' body. Then, as JESUS' hand falls downward . . .)

BLACKOUT

NARRATOR 2: *(During BLACKOUT)* When love is authentic, we desire what is best for our loved ones. Can we, with tearful joy, give them back to God? Back to the God, Who loaned them to us – even if only for a short while?

MUSIC INTERLUDE

(Lights still out as MARY sits with JESUS' body in her arms; she is between JOHN the APOSTLE (r) & MARY MAGDALENE & VERONICA, holding herbs (l) SIMON of CYRENE, holding Sign, stands behind JOHN. ETHAN & JOHANNA, hold burial cloth, at left. ANGELS form "arch" around MARY & JESUS. CAIAPHAS & SATANS at right LONGINIUS, CORNELIUS &

LUCAS at top center DISMAS & GESTAS remain on their Crosses. TIRA & remaining CAST, grieving, WOMEN holding flowers. JESUS' Cross is in stand at top center until the end of play.)

SCENE 25 REMOVAL FROM CROSS AND BURIAL

NARRATOR 2: Ethan, the Crossmaker, made countless crosses – instruments of torture for Rome's criminals. Today Ethan will provide an instrument of comfort.

(MARY removes Crown of Thorns. SIMON of CYRENE angrily looks at Sign & throws it aside. ANGELS assist ETHAN & JOHANNA in placing burial cloth over JESUS' body. TWO CHILDREN hug MARY. : ANGELS bow & SATANS jeer. VERONICA sprinkles herbs over JESUS' body.)
NARRATOR 2: Veronica's Veil comforted Jesus' painful face. Now, Veronica veils Jesus' Body with herbs--as was the practice—to preserve.

(MARY MAGDALENE and VERONICA argue over the placement of the burial cloths. JOHN the APOSTLE intervenes. MARY looks shocked.)

NARRATOR 2: Funerals sometimes bring out the worst in people. Families argue over who does what, or gets what. The Old Testament reminds us there is a season for everything. Do not disrespect the dead and each other with insensitive behavior.

(GUARDS cut DISMAS & GESTAS' down. SATANS approach & poke dead THIEVES' bodies like cats on a scratching post.)

NARRATOR 2:   Skeletons come out of closets at Funerals. Today is such day for Dismas, the Good Thief. His mother, Tira, realizes she knows someone else in the crowd.

(TIRA, holding flower, approaches DISMAS' body.)

NARRATOR 2:   Tira knew Longinius from years earlier when they had an affair. As she places a flower on Dismas' body, she is shocked to recognize Lucas as Longinius' son, the baby she left with the Centurion. Now grown up and a Centurion also.

(As TIRA places flower on DISMAS' body, LUCAS pushes her back.)

NARRATOR 1 *(as TIRA)*: Don't you dare push your mother!

NARRATOR 4 *(as LUCAS):* Woman, my mother is dead. Just ask my father. He's right over there.

(LONGINIUS arm-locks LUCAS. SATANS snicker).

NARRATOR 2:   Longinius realizes who the woman is and what she once meant to him.
NARRATOR 4 (as LONGINIUS): Lucas, I've made too many mistakes throughout my life. I killed an innocent man today! Please don't become what I am. Start over. It's not too late!

(LUCAS runs angrily out. TIRA shakes her head sadly at LONGINIUS and exits. LONGINIUS, stoically, remains in place.)

NARRATOR 2:   It's never too late for any of us. Life hands us thousands of chances to start again, all we have to do is choose one.

(ANGELS form "Honor Guard" behind MARY & JESUS. WOMEN & CHILDREN place flowers on JESUS' Body. SATANS gag, and then exit laughing. WOMEN & CHILDREN exit.   JOHN the APOSTLE places his hand on MARY'S shoulder.)

NARRATOR 2: From that day, on, John did as Jesus wished. He took Mary into his care as his own mother.

(SIMON of CYRENE steps forward to pay respect to MARY & JESUS, then exits.)

NARRATOR 2: What beauty can we return for the beauty of loving family members? It is thought that Simon of Cyrene became a disciple. At the end of the long Good Friday, he searches for the basket of eggs he lost... wondering if any could still be sold.

(SIMON of CYRENE finds egg basket.)

NARRATOR 2: But, to Simon's surprise, he finds a feast of intact eggs, gloriously colored! Thus, the tradition of coloring Eggs for Easter is born.

(SIMON of CYRENE shows audience the colored eggs as he exits.).

NARRATOR 2: Yet, love, and beauty are not recognized by everyone – they threaten those whose purpose is to degrade.
(GUARDS snicker & irreverently exit-as team mates. CORNELIUS, unable to look at MARY, stoically exits.)

NARRATOR 2: No one is beyond redemption, regardless of what they have done.

(LONGINIUS bows & removes helmet)

NARRATOR 2: As Jesus' life and teachings remind us-- all we need is to love, and to live out that love with our neighbor, as well as our self.

(MARY, with a gentle look, nods to LONGINIUS, who stares at MARY & exits. MARY MAGDALENE & VERONICA hug MARY & exit. JOHN the APOSTLE, holding two flowers, takes MARY's arm. JOHN places flower on JESUS' body & hands MARY a flower. MARY kisses her flower—raises flower to Heaven— ANGELS raise their "wings" then drop flower upon JESUS' covered body. JOHN and MARY exit. ANGELS remain as "guards" around JESUS' body. CAIAPHAS laughs as he proclaims…)

NARRATOR 4 *(as CAIAPHAS)*: HE'S DEAD!

(CAIAPHAS, laughing, exits. LIGHTS OUT.)

MUSICAL INTERLUDE BLACKOUT

SCENE 26   AN EMPTY TOMB/ RESURRECTION

(Lights still out. JESUS, JOHANNA & ETHAN at center; ANGEL GABRIEL between ANGELS; MICHAEL (r) and RAPHAEL (l) at center; JOHN the APOSTLE at right; MARY MAGDALENE at left . THIEVES' bodies, Crosses & stands are removed.)

NARRATOR 1: *(During BLACKOUT)* It is a chapter in our lives when we become caretakers. We are tied up with caring for another and we experience the pain of a different burial…the burial of our free schedule, the grave of a worried mind and fearful heart, the death of a life we once knew. But, caretakers who act in selfless love experience the promise of a rising to new life. What tombs are our lives in?

(LIGHTS UP)

(MARY MAGDALENE & JOHN the APOSTLE cautiously approach ANGEL GABRIEL.)

NARRATOR 4 *(as ANGEL GABRIEL)*: He is not here!

NARRATOR 1: Do we believe in the promise of eternal life, yet live, today, as if there was not one?

(MARY at center. CAST remains in place. JESUS' Burial Cloth is draped on the crossbeam of JESUS' Cross.)

MUSIC: HANDEL'S HALLELUIAH CHORUS

(JESUS comes down aisle. MARY MAGDALENE enters embraces/kisses JESUS.

NARRATOR 3 *(as MARY MAGDALENE):* Is it really You? Come with me. Peter and James will never believe me if they don't see you themselves.

(Cast bow and stand on either side of JESUS. LIGHTS OUT…EXCEPT one LIGHT that REMAINS on JESUS' CROSS at TOP CENTER)

NARRATOR 1: Ethan, the Crossmaker, became a disciple on that first Easter Morning. May we, too, not be afraid to take up our crosses, to go and make disciples of all nations as Jesus taught us. May we always believe, and want the Resurrection awaiting us all.
BLACKOUT, MUSICAL POSTLUDE, CAST CURTAIN CALL,

THE END

The Centurion

A Parish Passion Play

By Reverend Gerald Gurka,
M.Div.,MTh.,MA

Cast of Characters
Four narrators: two M, two F, will Voice the Characters

JESUS...The Son of God
MARY... Mother of Jesus
CORNELIUS................................Assistant Centurion
LONGINIUS................Head Centurion & Father of Lucas
LUCAS....................Young Guard, evil Son of Longinius
PONTIUS PILATE.................Roman Procurator of Judea
NERO.......................Dissolute, corrupt Roman Emperor
CLAUDIA PROCLES......................Wife of Pontius Pilate
SIMON OF CYRENE...........African farmer, helped Jesus
RUFUS.....................................Son of Simon of Cyrene
CAIAPHAS......... ..Jerusalem High Priest/Enemy of Jesus
JOHN.....................................Beloved Disciple of Jesus
JUDAS.......................... Treasurer of Disciples & Traitor
PETER..Head Disciple of Jesus
PERPETUA...Wife of Peter
SAREE...............................Daughter of Peter & Perpetua
MARY MAGDALENE.........Galilean Woman cured by Jesus
VERONICA..........................Used veil to wipe Jesus' face
MAIDSERVANT...........Young slave of Cornelius' household
JOANNA.....................................Secret Disciple of Jesus
SALOME.....................................Mother of John & James
REBECCA......................Daughter of Joseph of Arimathea
GESTAS' MOTHER....................Jerusalem drunk & harlot
WOMEN of JERUSALEM................Vigilantes for Criminals
ARCHANGEL GABRIEL..............God's Primary Messenger
ARCHANGEL MICHAEL..........Protector & Satan Adversary
ARCHANGEL RAPHAEL.............................God's Healer
GUARDIAN ANGELS...........................Messengers of God
MR. SATAN.......................Fallen Angel/Prince of Darkness

BOY SATAN............................Son of the Prince of Darkness
GIRLS............................Daughters of the Prince of Darkness
GUARDS....................................Assistants to the Centurions
SEBASTIAN....................................Roman Christian Athlete
BLIND YOUTH..Cured by Jesus
WATER BOYS..............................Young followers of Jesus
GESTAS................................Bad Thief crucified with Jesus
DISMAS........................ ...Good Thief crucified with Jesus
JOHN THE ....Cousin/Forerunner of Jesus
CANDLEBEARER...............................Early Christian Convert
CHLOE.....................................Early Christian Godmother
SILAS...Early Christian Godfather

NARRATORS: Master Storyteller, Conscience of Cornelius,
"Voices" of   Main Characters

CREW: CROSS DESIGN, LIGHTING DESIGN, SOUND DESIGN,
MUSIC, HAIR & MAKEUP DESIGN, COS-
TUMES, PROPS, GREETERS & REFRESHMENTS

SETTING: Rome: During Emperor Nero's reign; a time of Christian
Persecution and gladiator fights, Jerusalem: Passover Week...from
Palm Sunday to Easter Sunday.

A NOTE from the AUTHOR: Ideally, this play should be presented in a
church; Making use of the sanctuary/altar area. Because each Church
has a different layout, stage directions are simple: enter, exit, left, right,
aisle, altar, etc.

LIGHTS: Spot lights with color gels; Optional: Strobe, and fog
machines. A dimmer to raise and lower lights, and fog machine.
Backdrop, or projection of Roman Coliseum

MUSIC: Pre-recorded. Church Choir & Instrumentalists; or combination thereof.

DIRECTOR'S WELCOME ADDRESS
(SPOTLIGHT UP. DIRECTOR at Front. Welcomes audience.

BLACKOUT

INTRODUCTION

(Lights still out. SEBASTIAN, tied to post, stripped of his garments & riddled with arrows, at Center. CORNELIUS, holding bow & arrow, with LUCAS at left, LYSANDER and ANGELS at right. SATANS, MAGNUS & DECIMUS, holding bows, at front.)

NARRATOR: It was a time of Christian persecution. The Emperor Nero's hedonistic lifestyle continued to catapult Rome into debt. Nero especially hated Christians because their lifestyle challenged him to a conversion he did not want to face. Secretly, Nero planned to rid the city of Rome from any Christian influence. He blamed the Christians for the fire which destroyed a large section of Rome. In reality, Nero sent his Centurions, as arsonists…wanting this section of the city for his own purpose: to build a shopping center for his wife—and to have a direct view of the Coliseum, from the portico of his palace—so that he could watch the gladiator games from the comfort of his home. And, in the Coliseum, Christians were made sport of—losing their lives battling lions and tigers. Nero especially delighted in watching his well-trained gladiators fight the Christians to their death. He took special pride in four gladiators who were also centurions.

SCENE 1   THE MURDER of SEBASTIAN

LIGHTS UP

NARRATOR: Nero's centurions, Cornelius, Lucas, Lysander, Magnus and Decimus were friends. *(LYSANDER confidently smiling, bows to audience, MAGNUS, snarling, bows to audience, DECIMUS, angrily, bows to audience)* They also were gladiators. But, at this very moment, Cornelius was having second thoughts about his job.

(CORNELIUS, visibly shaken, aims arrow at SEBASTIAN but cannot release the arrow from its bow.)

NARRATOR: Lucas screamed at Cornelius *(LUCAS approaches, slaps CORNELIUS' hand).*

VOICE OF LUCAS: "Shoot him! Let's get this over with one right through his heart.

(CORNELIUS shakes & cannot release the arrow. LYSANDER, MAGNUS & DECIMUS laugh. LUCAS becomes enraged.)

NARRATOR: The thoughts which filled Cornelius' mind were not of killing, but of a wise teacher named Jesus, who miraculously healed his maid servant. *(LUCAS shouts into CORNELIUS' ear.)* Cornelius heard Lucas shout, "Old man, are you hard of hearing? What's wrong with you? Sebastian is nothing but a traitor. We can't have an emperor's guard who loves and protects Christians!" But Cornelius could not shoot an assassinating arrow into Sebastian.

(LYSANDER approaches LUCAS inquiring "what's with Cornelius?")

VOICE OF LUCAS: Shoot the arrow! He deserves death!
(CORNELIUS does not release the arrow. LUCAS shoves his face into CORNELIUS' face.)

NARRATOR: Cornelius spat on the ground and then yelled at Lucas: "I have had enough of killing! *(CORNELIUS throws down his bow & arrow.)* I haven't slept a night since we murdered all those innocent babies under that sicko Herod! I should never have taken a part in Jesus' Crucifixion! And then Nero ordering us to burn down Rome--I could still smell the burning flesh! I will not take another life of an innocent person!"

(LUCAS stops CORNELIUS.)

VOICE OF LUCAS: Why you're nothing but another sniveling traitor. If you don't finish Sebastian off—I WILL! AND NERO WILL HEAR ABOUT THIS! *(MR. SATAN hands LUCAS a club. Mr. SATAN laughs. LUCAS clubs SEBASTIAN, to death. MAGNUS, LYSANDER & DECIMUS laugh. ANGELS, weeping, approach SEBASTIAN)*

BLACKOUT

SCENE 2   CORNELIUS at the COLISEUM

(Lights are still out. NERO Center, CORNELIUS, with sword, Front of altar LYSANDER, MAGNUS & DECIMUS, with swords behind altar. LUCAS, holding sword, at Back)

NARRATOR: *(During BLACKOUT)* Cornelius had no way of knowing that years from now, another guard in the Roman Praetorian— also a Christian in secret, named Sebastian—would meet the same fate during the reign of the anti-Christian emperor Diocletian. But, now, instead of seeing the future, all Cornelius could envision was his past— and his participation in Jesus' Crucifixion upon a cross.

(LIGHTS UP)

NARRATOR: Lucas reported Cornelius' insubordination to Nero. *(LUCAS comes down aisle.)* It gave Nero great delight to make a public spectacle of anyone who was a Christian sympathizer—even if that sympathizer was Cornelius the Assistant Roman Centurion. *(LUCAS spits at CORNELIUS.)*

NARRATOR: Nero saw great profit to be made in having the Assistant Centurion of Rome battle his comrades. Nero exploited their friendship and sold tickets for their fight to the death in the Roman Coliseum. *(NERO raises his hand and then rapidly lowers it)*

NARRATOR: Nero shouted, "Let the Games begin!"

(LYSANDER and CORNELIUS battle: LYSANDER'S sword cuts CORNELIUS' forearm. LYSANDER moves in for the kill, raising his sword. CORNELIUS stabs LYSANDER in the abdomen. LYSANDER falls to ground. DECIMUS raises his sword over his head. They battle. CORNELIUS' sword slices the side of DECIMUS' throat. As DECIMUS collapses, MAGNUS and CORNELIUS battle. CORNELIUS plunges his sword into MAGNUS' side. MAGNUS falls to his knees, groveling for help. LUCAS, angrily challenges CORNELIUS. They fiercely battle. LUCAS strikes CORNELIUS across the back. CORNELIUS falls to ground   MAGNUS crawls toward CORNELIUS. LUCAS slices his sword across CORNELIUS' back. CORNELIUS falls to ground. LUCAS raises his sword high, ready for the killer strike.)

NARRATOR: Lucas mocked Cornelius, "Let's see if your Jesus will save you now!"
BLACKOUT

SCENE 3   JESUS' BAPTISM

(Lights still out. CORNELIUS at right. JOHN the BAPTIST & ANGELS at Top Center   JESUS at right.   A container of water is near JOHN the BAPTIST.)

NARRATOR: *(During BLACKOUT, as LUCAS raises his sword high for the killer strike.)* The past few years of Cornelius' life began to flash before his eyes; to the very first time he saw Jesus. It was at the Jordan River. And Jesus was being baptized by his cousin John, whom everyone called "The Baptist."

(LIGHTS up. JESUS embraces JOHN the BAPTIST. JESUS kneels before JOHN the BAPTIST who shakes his head NO! JESUS nods "yes" to JOHN the BAPTIST who pours water over JESUS. ANGELS raise their wings.)

NARRATOR: Cornelius remembered that, as John baptized Jesus, a voice could be heard echoing throughout the heavens. It was a very loving voice, -which said, "This is my beloved Son with whom I am well pleased."
(JESUS raises his hands up. CORNELIUS, curiously, approaches JESUS)

NARRATOR: Cornelius knew that he felt an attraction to John's message: to welcome the Messiah by living life with a pure and clean heart. Cornelius knew that he desired to leave his sinful ways behind.

BLACKOUT

SCENE 4   PALM SUNDAY

(Lights are still out. ENTIRE CAST holding palms. JESUS in Front of altar is between MARY, MARY MAGDALENE, JOHN the APOSTLE, VERONICA & JUDAS, PETER, ANGELS, YOUNG GIRL & MOTHER. RUFUS & SIMON of CYRENE at Center. YOUNG CHILD WITH BANDAGE & MOTHER at left front. WOMEN of JERUSALEM at right front CORNELIUS at Center. CAIAPHAS far right/ SATANS behind CAIAPHAS; LONGINIUS, LUCAS, GUARDS at Center)

NARRATOR: *(During BLACKOUT)* However, Cornelius did not believe that he was worthy enough to follow the Messiah. His participation in the murder of the Holy Innocents never left his mind...and from this grew a terrible anger and self-hatred. As an army captain, Cornelius felt caught between two loyalties: his loyalty to Rome and the Italian Regiment under his command; as well as his loyalty to his neighboring Jews in Caesarea, which was Cornelius' hometown. Caesarea was located in the volatile region of Palestine. Here, Cornelius and his fellow guards were stationed to keep the peace. Cornelius' peers often made fun of him--for not participating in the debaucheries of orgies and wine festivals--which were held in honor of the pagan gods.

(LIGHTS UP)

NARRATOR: It was a Sunday afternoon when Cornelius had his first conversation with Jesus. Upon seeing Jesus at the gate of Jerusalem, Cornelius was intrigued at seeing a mother bring her child to Jesus. (*YOUNG GIRL & MOTHER run to Jesus; He hugs her. ANGELS raise their wings.*) Cornelius noticed that upon Jesus' face was an illumination which he never saw on any face before. (*RUFUS starts coming down aisle. SIMON, angrily, shouting at RUFUS follows*)

NARRATOR: Cornelius also saw another child...a young boy approach Jesus. The young boy's father was shouting at him...but it soon became apparent to Cornelius that this young boy was deaf. (*RUFUS kneels in front of JESUS. ANGELS wave their wings. RAPHAEL places her hand on the boy's shoulder RUFUS hugs JESUS*) After greeting the boy, Jesus spit into the palms of His hands and placed his hands upon the child's ears.

(*RUFUS rises with a smile-filled wonderment on his face, then places his hands to his ears. Cornelius came to realize that Jesus had miraculously healed the young boy's hearing. YOUNG CHILD with BANDAGE & MOTHER approach JESUS.)*

NARRATOR: A third child with a bandage wrapped about his head, approached Jesus. His mother followed. Jesus hugged the child and gently removed the bandage

(RAPHAEL places hand upon the CHILD'S shoulder as JESUS removes bandage & throws to ground. ANGELS wave wings high.)

NARRATOR: Cornelius could never forget the look upon the child's face when she realized that she could now see.

(MOTHER hugs JESUS; SATANS, look repulsed, approach JESUS; CORNELIUS starts down aisle.)

NARRATOR: Sensing a divine love, Cornelius, somehow, got the courage to approach Jesus. But when he came near the Messiah, a man known as Judas used a palm branch to stop him.

(JUDAS slaps the palm across CORNELIUS' chest. PETER approaches CORNELIUS. CAIAPHAS, revolting, slowly approaches JESUS.)

NARRATOR: Then, a man named Peter said, "Don't bother the Messiah, you're a pagan soldier, leave him alone. But Jesus interrupted and asked, "Cornelius, what is it you want of me?" Cornelius was incredulous, for Jesus knew his name without asking! *(CORNELIUS, angrily, notices CAIAPHAS. ANGELS look toward CAIAPHAS and shudder.)*

NARRATOR: Upon seeing Caiaphas, Cornelius' stomach began to churn. For Cornelius often overhead Caiaphas ranting that this Jesus—who claims to be the Messiah—must be stopped. Cornelius bowed and knelt before Jesus, saying: "Master Teacher, I know of your reputation. I believe in the love and concern you preach. My maid servant is ill and in great need of healing. I will be grateful in whatever way you can assist."

(ANGELS wave wings high. RAPHAEL bows towards JESUS. JESUS, smiling, places his hands upon CORNELIUS' shoulders.)

VOICE of JESUS: Go in peace, your maid servant will be healed.

(CORNELIUS rises & gratefully grasps JESUS' hands. JUDAS looks at CORNELIUS with repulsion. SATANS point their fingers into their mouths with a "gag-me" gesture.)

NARRATOR: Cornelius often thought of this moment—the very moment his maid servant's health was restored.

(CORNELIUS walks down Center Aisle. MARY looks at JESUS with great pride. MARY MAGDALENE, holding palm, begins to dance in front of JESUS & then "dances" down Center Aisle. ENTIRE CAST begins waving palm branches and pieces of material "dance/circle/bow" around JESUS, leading him down Center Aisle. CAST reacts with Audience inviting them to honor JESUS. JUDAS, jealously, remains in Front of altar, throws palm to ground. CAIAPHAS & SATANS remain in their places; they angrily react.)

SCENE 5   JUDAS SELLS JESUS

(CAIAPHAS, "tip-toes," to JUDAS. SATANS "slither" behind JUDAS.)

NARRATOR: Cornelius heard the revelry behind him. A joyful satisfaction overcame him...a joyful peace that Jesus was being honored as if a new king had come to visit Jerusalem. Not until later that week would he learn the plot that Caiaphas and Judas were now planning. *(SATANS throw coins "showering" JUDAS.)* Cornelius had heard that Judas was the treasurer of Jesus' disciples. But, Cornelius would never imagine the moral bankruptcy that now occurred. *(CAIAPHAS swings a money pouch before JUDAS' eyes.)* Caiaphas tempted Judas to betray Jesus for 30 pieces of silver.

(SATANS drop & catch coins before JUDAS who, unsuccessfully tries to capture the coins. CAIAPHAS motions "Let's not be greedy!")

NARRATOR: Walking into Jerusalem, Cornelius recalled the many rumors that were spread about Judas and Jesus; that Judas was jealous of Jesus' success with the crowds; *(CAIAPHAS, gleefully, dangles money pouch closer to JUDAS)*, and that Judas wanted Jesus to be a more domineering Messiah; that Judas wanted Jesus to use his miraculous powers to overthrow the ruling powers.

(JUDAS reaches out to shake CAIAPHAS' hand & snatches the money pouch. JUDAS & CAIAPHAS enter Center Aisle, walking down like team mates. SATANS, applauding, approach JUDAS & CAIAPHAS. JUDAS happily displays coins to Audience gesturing: "Look! I've got the Money!" CAIAPHAS halts at Center Aisle Middle. JUDAS continues walking down aisle. SATANS follow gesturing "loser" sign.)

BLACKOUT

NARRATOR: *(During BLACKOUT)* As Cornelius recalled these rumors, a gnawing sense of discomfort overcame him; a foreboding perception that he was about to become intermingled in an unwarranted mess.

SCENE 6   THE SHOPKEEPERS: SILAS & CHLOE

(Lights still out. CORNELIUS, SILAS & CHLOE at Center with   LUCAS, PETER, PERPETUA and SAREE. JESUS, holding pitcher, & JUDAS, holding wash bowl/towel in Front of altar. MARY, MARY MAGDALENE, VERONICA, JOHN the APOSTLE, YOUNG CHILDREN, ANGELS, SATANS at sides. Cloth, Candles, dish with bread & cup set on altar)

NARRATOR: *(During BLACKOUT)* Acknowledging these discomforting feelings, Cornelius rationed that it's no secret: most of Palestine knows that Judas Iscariot loves money. Cornelius mused that if Judas had children he probably would even sell them if a profit were to be made. Most likely, Judas is using this position as Jesus' treasurer to advance his career. Judas should have stayed in Kerioth, where he came from. With this thought, Cornelius began shopping in Jerusalem in preparation for the Passover supper. He was looking forward to being with his family for this coming Thursday Night's Feast. *(CORNELIUS starts down aisle)*

(LIGHTS UP)

NARRATOR: *(female voice)* Cornelius entered our market to make arrangements for purchasing the Passover Lamb. My husband Silas and I could see that Cornelius was very excited about Jesus' entrance into Jerusalem.

NARRATOR: *(male voice)* Cornelius told my wife Chloe how Jesus assured him that his maid servant would be healed. Cornelius was so trusting that what Jesus said would come true. I looked into Chloe's eyes *(SILAS nods to CHLOE)*, and at that very moment I knew that we both sensed that Cornelius desired to become a disciple of Jesus.

NARRATOR: *(female voice)* But I sensed that there was a lot of fear inside Cornelius—especially when the young guard Lucas stormed into our shop. *(LUCAS approaches CORNELIUS)*. All of Jerusalem gossiped about this young, very handsome guard. But his beautiful looks betrayed him—for I believe that Lucas would sell his soul in order to become a Centurion. Arrogantly, *(LUCAS slaps CORNELIUS' shoulder.)* I heard Lucas tell Cornelius that Longinius, the Head Centurion, was ordering him and Cornelius to work throughout the Passover Holiday...that Cornelius would not be able to return home to be with his family. *(CORNELIUS angrily looks at LUCAS)*. Lucas also told Cornelius that it was Caiaphas, the High Priest, who was responsible for ordering all Centurions and guards to report for active duty throughout this holiday weekend. (LUCAS exits to Center Aisle Back   CHLOE shudders. *PETER, PERPETUA, SAREE approach CHLOE & SILAS*) As Lucas left--our shop suddenly felt as if it were covered with ice.

NARRATOR: *(male voice)* When Peter and his wife Perpetua walked into our shop, with their daughter Saree, I noticed how enthused Cornelius became. I heard Cornelius ask Peter many questions about Jesus our Master Teacher.

BLACKOUT

SCENE 7   THE LAST SUPPER

(Lights are still out. JESUS, holding water pitcher, JUDAS, holding wash bowl with towel, & PETER are in Front of altar.   MARY, MARY MAGDALENE, JOHN the APOSTLE, VERONICA, YOUNG CHILDREN, SILAS, CHLOE, SAREE at altar ANGELS at Top Center   SATANS at right front   Candles, lighted, Cup & Dish with bread are placed upon Altar.)

NARRATOR: *(During BLACKOUT)* Upon leaving the market, Cornelius saw Lucas smiling at the young women who flocked around him.

Instantly, Cornelius remembered that this was the same smile which always seemed to paint Lucas' face whenever Lucas would kill his opponent, in the games at the Coliseum. And, with this thought, Cornelius wondered about the numerous families whose tables, this coming Passover, would now have empty chairs where their loved ones once sat. Profound guilt and shame began to invade Cornelius as he now admitted, to himself, that he, Lucas, and his fellow Centurions and Guards were responsible for killing so many.

NARRATOR: As Cornelius walked through the streets of Jerusalem he wondered how Jesus, the Master Teacher, would celebrate his Passover Meal. *(LIGHTS UP)* Within a week, Cornelius would come to learn that Jesus, the Master Teacher, would wash the feet of his disciples before they sat down to eat.

(JESUS attempts to wash PETER'S feet   PETER refuses, staying JESUS' arm. JUDAS scoffs, putting the wash bowl down)

NARRATOR: When Peter refused to have his feet washed, Judas became angry and accused Peter of false humility. *(JESUS picks up wash bowl)* Yet, Peter agreed to have his feet washed when Jesus explained that this was necessary...if Peter wanted to feed his flock of believers. *(JESUS washes PETER'S feet; together, they exit. JUDAS scoffs. ANGELS go to Center.)*

NARRATOR: At the table, while sharing the Passover Meal with his disciples, Jesus took the bread. Said the Blessing, broke the bread and gave it to his disciples saying:

VOICE of JESUS: Take it. This is My Body.

(JESUS raises the bread for all to see.   ANGELS bow then raise their wings toward JESUS. SATANS, using their arms, shield their faces.)

NARRATOR: Then Jesus took the cup and gave thanks. Jesus said to his apostles:

VOICE of JESUS: This is the blood of the new covenant that will be shed for many. Do this in memory of Me.

(JESUS raises the cup for all to see. ANGELS bow & raise wings; SATANS mock, gesturing: "Let's drink to each other!" When JESUS places cup upon table, JOHN the APOSTLE leans his head upon JESUS' chest; JUDAS looks at JOHN the APOSTLE with disgust. PETER, angrily, approaches JUDAS.)

NARRATOR: Cornelius would also learn that--after Jesus distributed the bread and wine—an argument arose between Peter and Judas.

(PETER grabs JUDAS'S shoulders; MARY approaches PETER begging him to let JUDAS alone. MARY MAGDALENE approaches MARY.)

NARRATOR: Jesus' mother, Mary, sensed the anguish within Judas' heart. As the loving Mother of all the disciples, Mary sensed that Judas needed some motherly affection.

(MARY embraces JUDAS. JUDAS, lovingly yet fearfully, looks at MARY. MARY MAGDALENE, angrily, stares at JUDAS. ANGELS bow toward MARY.)

NARRATOR: However, Mary had no idea of the beats of betrayal which were within Judas' heart.

(SATANS, "squirming" to attention, approach JUDAS. BOY SATAN, using pitchfork, pokes JUDAS in the back. JUDAS breaks away from MARY'S embrace. JESUS approaches JUDAS, and tries to grasp his hands; JUDAS resists & walks away.)

NARRATOR: Mary and the apostles saw the raw disappointment which washed Jesus' face; they did not notice the confusion and shame which painted Judas' every step away from the table.

(BOY SATAN, laughing, pushes JUDAS forward. SATANS follow, cheering JUDAS. ANGELS weep.)

NARRATOR: Cornelius would learn that Judas expected Jesus to be a political Messiah, who would relieve the heavy burden of Roman taxation, rather than a spiritual Messiah, who would relieve the heavy burdens of one's soul and heart.

(JUDAS, looking back towards JESUS, walks down aisle with SATANS; who huddle around him as their "star player." JESUS reaches out to JUDAS; CAST follows JESUS. MARY places her head upon JESUS' shoulder. MR. SATAN, looking back, snickers at JESUS. SATANS turn back, making the "Loser-sign" toward JESUS.)

BLACKOUT   MUSIC INTERLUDE

NARRATOR: *(During BLACKOUT)* Upon finishing the Passover Meal, Jesus and His disciples sang a hymn to thank God the Father for His continued blessing.

SCENE 8   THE GARDEN

(Lights are still out. JESUS, facing Audience, is between JOHN the APOSTLE and PETER, with sword, at Front of altar. ANGELS at Center. LONGINIUS, LUCAS, GUARDS at right, CONRAD at left. JUDAS, CORNELIUS, CAIAPHAS & SATANS in Back)

NARRATOR: *(During BLACKOUT)* Judas had informed Caiaphas that, often after sharing a meal, Jesus would love to take him and his fellow disciples to a Garden of Olive trees which was located on a mount in Gethsemane. There, Jesus taught them how to meditate and pray.

(LIGHTS UP. JESUS, prayerfully, raises his hands up. JOHN the APOSTLE & PETER yawn, falling asleep to ground. ANGELS extend their arms towards JESUS.)

NARRATOR: I, Cornelius, was the lucky one, chosen by Longinius, the Head Centurion, to escort Judas. As we waited among the olive trees, I hated being the Centurion who would escort a disciple to betray his Master Teacher—especially when that Master Teacher was Jesus—the very person who healed my maid servant. As we waited, I resented hearing Caiaphas tell Judas that he had performed a noble service for the Roman Empire by handing over Jesus to the authorities. I hated even more the sniveling chuckle which accompanied Caiaphas' every word.

(JUDAS, CORNELIUS & SATANS start down aisle; CAIAPHAS, cautiously, follows. LONGINIUS, LUCAS, GUARDS approach JESUS; CORNELIUS stays near altar)

NARRATOR: *(As JUDAS approaches Altar)* As we approached Jesus, I noticed that the sweat upon Jesus' forehead had turned into drops of blood which, in the moonlight, glistened upon his brow...they crashed to the earth like a cardinal which lost its wings.

(JESUS, deep in prayer, walks to Center; once there, JESUS' back is toward Audience. ANGEL MICHAEL places his hand on JESUS' shoulder. JUDAS halts in Front of altar; CAIAPHAS pushes JUDAS forward and "slithers" to Right. LUCAS, angrily, approaches CORNELIUS. LONGINIUS & GUARDS raise high their weapons. SATANS, walking towards altar, rub their hands together, as if twigs starting a fire. MR..SATAN shoves JUDAS into JESUS. JUDAS betrays JESUS with a "kiss:" lays his head on JESUS' shoulder.

JESUS turns around. JUDAS exits. LONGINIUS orders GUARDS to capture JESUS. PETER & JOHN the APOSTLE awaken. GUARDS throw JESUS to ground. SATANS mock: "oops!" PETER, frozen, stands watching. LUCAS hits JOHN the APOSTLE who falls to ground. LUCAS steps on JOHN'S garment, raises sword. CORNELIUS stops LUCAS. PETER, raises his sword, approaches LUCAS. JOHN rises; escaping to right. JOHN'S garment, caught under LUCAS' foot rips away. SATANS, mocking, cover their eyes yet peek through their fingers at JOHN the APOSTLE. LUCAS, laughing, approaches JESUS. PETER raises his sword, severing CORNELIUS' ear. PETER escapes left. JESUS rises, places his hand upon CORNELIUS' severed ear, healing it. SATANS pretend to regurgitate. CORNELIUS & JESUS stare intently at each other. LUCAS, angrily gestures to LONGINIUS to "capture" JESUS. LONGINIUS, GUARDS, then LUCAS, beat JESUS, tie JESUS' hands together and exit. SATANS stamp their pitchforks in victory; ANGELS RAPHAEL, MICHAEL & GABRIEL follow JESUS. ANGELS remain at place where JESUS prayed. As JESUS & GUARDS walk down aisle, CAIAPHAS, "tip-toes" to Front altar looking towards JESUS; CAIAPHAS gloats. CONRAD approaches CAIAPHAS.)

NARRATOR: Journeying through the area was a wise man named Conrad. He approached Caiaphas asking, "I have heard that the new Messiah-King is here in Jerusalem. By your clothes, I can see that you are a religious leader. *(CONRAD bows to CAIAPHAS.)* Would you please tell me where I can find this Messiah-King?" *(CAIAPHAS snickers then loudly laughs.)*

NARRATOR: Caiaphas replied to Conrad, "Who gave you that information? There has never been a new Messiah, here, in Jerusalem!" *(CAIAPHAS, pleased, walks down Center Aisle. CONRAD, perplexed, looks into the Audience, then walks into Center Aisle and stops.)*

BLACKOUT

NARRATOR: *(During BLACKOUT)* Thirty-three years ago, Conrad traveled with three fellow Wise Men to Bethlehem in search of the new born King. Deterred by teenage robbers, Conrad became separated from his fellow Magi. Nevertheless, Conrad never abandoned his quest to meet this new king. And, for these past thirty-three years, the look of youth had never abandoned Conrad—for some miraculous reason, unlike the other three Wise Men, Conrad never continued to age.

SCENE 9   PETER'S DENIAL

(Lights still out. PETER at Center, CONRAD at left, CORNELIUS at altar. WOMAN of JERUSALEM at right, JUDAS at Center; CAIAPHAS at right.)

NARRATOR: Conrad decided to follow Caiaphas and the crowd that carried away the man whom Conrad saw praying in the garden. Conrad was hoping that someone in the crowd would be able to provide information that would enable him to finally meet the Messiah King, for whom Conrad had been searching all these years. Conrad did not know that the man he saw praying, in the garden, was the one he had been searching for--- Jesus—the new Messiah-King

NARRATOR: *(During BLACKOUT)* While on the way to where the chief priests and the entire Sanhedrin would gather, Cornelius and Conrad saw how Lucas, Longinius and the Guards continued to club, mock and spit at Jesus *(SOUND EFFECT: Moaning);* even pushing him down an embankment; forcing him to climb back to the road. Following Conrad.at a distance was Peter.

NARRATOR: *(During BLACKOUT)* Upon reaching their destination, the guards took Jesus inside to meet where Caiaphas the high priest, and the scribes and elders would be assembled.

(LIGHTS UP. PETER, shivering, warms himself, at Center; CORNELIUS looks into Audience, CONRAD approaches slowly)

NARRATOR: Peter, Cornelius and Conrad waited in the courtyard. As they stood in the chill of the night, they watched as people entered and exited the courtyard. Cornelius, Peter and Conrad heard people laughing and bragging about the money they could make bringing false testimony against Jesus of Nazareth.

(WOMAN OF JERUSALEM approaches PETER)
NARRATOR: Cornelius, Peter and Conrad heard the voices of the High Priest traveling beyond the window: "Jesus has blasphemed! He deserves to die!" Cornelius saw one of the maids approach Peter and say: "You were with Jesus! I saw you! You're one of His disciples!"
(WOMAN of JERUSALEM points her finger at PETER.)

NARRATOR: In a loud voice Peter denied this woman's accusations. *(PETER gestures: "NO!")* Seeing the frightened look upon Peter's face, Cornelius was certain that Peter was the disciple whose sword dismembered his ear in the garden just a few hours ago. Cornelius said to Peter, "Surely you are Jesus' disciple! I saw you in the Garden. It was your sword that..."
(PETER violently gestures "NO!")

NARRATOR: But Peter would not allow Cornelius to finish. Peter began to curse and swear at Cornelius. *(CONRAD approaches PETER.)*

NARRATOR: While Peter was swearing, Conrad came and said to Peter: "I overheard the Centurion. He's right; it was you in the garden!"
(PETER, like a "caged animal" gestures: "NO!)

NARRATOR: Peter shouted at Conrad, "I was not there!" Cornelius replied, "Yes YOU WERE! IT WAS YOUR SWORD THAT CUT OFF

MY EAR!" Peter stomped and shouted, "I TELL YOU-- I DO NOT KNOW THE MAN!"

(SOUND EFFECT: Cock crowing)

NARRATOR: As Peter proclaimed his denial, Cornelius heard a cock begin to crow...and as the cock crowed, Peter ran from the courtyard.

(PETER exits, running CONRAD & CORNELIUS stare at each other; and exit. JUDAS comes down aisle. CAIAPHAS at Center.)

SCENE 10   JUDAS' REFUND

(RUFUS at left, SATANS at right; GIRL SATAN is holding a noose.)

NARRATOR: It was now morning. Judas never wanted Jesus to be condemned; he bitterly regretted what he had done. In haste he went to return the thirty pieces of silver to the chief priests and elders. *(JUDAS walks to Front of altar. RUFUS enters.)*

NARRATOR: But, before Judas could enter the high priests' quarters, a boy named Rufus, came ran to him saying, "My dad, Simon, said that you are one of Jesus' disciples; and that you know where Jesus is! I want to thank Jesus and tell him how great it is that I can hear!" *(JUDAS, in disbelief, stares at RUFUS. CAIAPHAS, snickering approaches JUDAS & RUFUS)*

NARRATOR: Caiaphas said to Rufus, "This man Judas is wonderful at letting people know who Jesus is! I'll make sure Jesus gets your message. Now run along and play with your pigs, or whatever animals you have in your yard!"

(CAIAPHAS waves his hands in dismissal at RUFUS who exits running. JUDAS approaches CAIAPHAS; glares & throws money back at CAIAPHAS. CAIAPHAS laughs. SATANS approach JUDAS. GIRL SATAN is swinging the noose; she taps Mr. SATAN on shoulder, hands him the noose.)

NARRATOR: Judas did not believe that he could be forgiven by Jesus. *(JUDAS, terrified, walks down aisle & speaking: "I shouldn't have done it. BOY SATAN takes JUDAS' hand, starts petting JUDAS' hand.)*

NARRATOR: Gossips throughout Jerusalem claimed that Judas could not forgive himself for having been abused as a child.

(GIRL SATAN approaches JUDAS & caresses JUDAS' face.)

NARRATOR: The gossips also claimed that Judas, himself, was a child abuser. *(JUDAS leaps into the air screaming: "NO! LET ME ALONE!" MR. SATAN places noose around JUDAS' neck. JUDAS stares at SATANS, who laugh at him. SATANS flash the "loser" sign at JUDAS.)*

BLACKOUT

NARRATOR: *(During BLACKOUT)* Judas would not allow the Light of Christ to touch his pain. In a putrid spot, Judas hung himself from a tree. It is said that, after his death, Judas' body burst open; spewing his entrails, *(SOUND EFFECT: CROWS)* which were eaten by black birds of prey.

SCENE 11   THE TRIAL

(Lights still out. PONTIUS PILATE, CLAUDIA, LONGINIUS, CORNELIUS & JESUS, with hands tied, LUCAS at Center Aisle Back   GUARDS between GESTAS (r) & DISMAS (l) at Front of altar MARY, MARY MAGDALENE, JOHN the APOSTLE at left; SATANS, with bottles, whips, crown of thorns, red cloak, water bowl, near front pew. ANGELS at left front. A palm branch is

placed on floor at left. Crosses for GESTAS & DISMAS are at left & right front.
Cross for JESUS is Center.)

NARRATOR:*(During BLACKOUT)* As Cornelius and Longinius escorted
Jesus to his trial before Pontius Pilate; Cornelius looked at Jesus
knowing not what to say. He could not find words which would
adequately capture his gratitude to Jesus...for not only healing his
maid servant—but, now for restoring his ear...as if no blade had
murdered his hearing. Further regret filled Cornelius as he overheard
the plans that Caiaphas and procurator Pontius Pilate were now
making...plans for a crucifixion even though it was Passover. Cornelius
knew that, after Passover, three criminals were scheduled to be
executed: Barabbas and his younger cohorts Dismas and Gestas.
Cornelius was well aware that Barabbas collected homeless children
and introduced them to a life of crime. Like a master pimp, Barabbas
profited from itchy, youthful fingers.

(LIGHTS UP. GESTAS, flexing his muscles & GUARD walk to right. SATAN
GIRLS admire GESTAS' muscles.)

NARRATOR: Thirty some years ago, in Bethlehem, Barabbas found
the infant Gestas abandoned at his doorstep. Barabbas had known
Gestas' mother quite well; she was one of many women from
Barabbas' stable. Gestas' mother used her son as payment to
Barabbas, for money she owed; a payment for an ill-begotten addiction.
Barabbas raised Gestas in the very image of his crooked self.

(DISMAS, looking shameful, & GUARD walk to left front   MR. SATAN &
BOY SATAN, gesturing "loser" sign, approach DISMAS.)

NARRATOR: Gestas befriended a youth named Dismas. It was
rumored that Dismas was the illegitimate son of Longinius the Head
Centurion. And, since Longinius possessed no love for Dismas' mother.

whose name was Tira, she had no love for him. The only affection Dismas knew was from the household of Barabbas; and the tutorial attention of an older youth named Gestas.

(PONTIUS PILATE, escorted by LONGINIUS, & CLAUDIA, escorted by CORNELIUS, enter.)

NARRATOR: Cornelius knew Pontius Pilate to be a man of extreme pride as well as extreme meanness. Excessively superstitious, Pilate and his wife, Claudia, lived in the same dwelling that housed the mad king, Herod. Cornelius believed that Pilate's wife, Claudia, would make a better leader than her husband. *(PONTIUS PILATE & CLAUDIA, between LONGINIUS (l) & CORNELIUS (r), walk to Center)*

NARRATOR: Cornelius heard Claudia beg her husband to give Jesus His freedom. Cornelius was also hoping that Pilate would free Jesus-- the man who healed his maid-servant –the man who, while being arrested, took time to miraculously heal his ear. However, Cornelius was well-aware that Caiaphas and his henchmen had paid many of Jerusalem's derelicts to infiltrate the Praetorium crowd; and, be ready to shout that Jesus should be crucified.

(LUCAS shoves JESUS down aisle. When JESUS reaches altar, ANGELS RAPHAEL & MICHAEL approach JESUS: RAPHAEL bows to JESUS & MICHAEL places hands, as if blessing, over JESUS.)

NARRATOR: Electrifying guilt and shame overwhelmed Cornelius for not speaking up for Jesus…Cornelius feared the harm which Pilate might inflict upon him and his family. Cornelius began to sink into a tidal wave of bitterness.

(LUCAS pushes JESUS to Top Center; LUCAS spits at JESUS.)

NARRATOR: However, despite all the beatings Jesus endured, Cornelius saw that there was no bitterness, no anger, nor resentment in Jesus. Instantly, Cornelius remembered last night—in the courtyard-- and wondered why Peter would not admit that he was a disciple of Jesus. In a low voice, Cornelius questioned; "Where are the other disciples of Jesus? Where are all the people that Jesus healed?"

(LONGINIUS, angrily, stares at CORNELIUS, as LONGINIUS stares at MARY, JOHN the APOSTLE, & MARY MAGDALENE approach the altar; ANGEL GABRIEL, with outstretched arms, follows them.)

NARRATOR: Cornelius sensed that Pilate was afraid of becoming unpopular with the crowd. An angry hatred for his job began to consume Cornelius when Pilate ordered him, Longinius and Lucas to scourge Jesus—in the hope that the mob would throw a sympathy vote--and release Jesus. For it was the custom, on the occasion of the feast, to release one prisoner.

(PONTIUS PILATE commands CENTURIONS & GUARDS to scourge JESUS.   LONGINIUS & CORNELIUS approach JESUS. LONGINIUS pushes Him to floor. LUCAS, laughing, kicks JESUS. CLAUDIA, with disgust, looks at PILATE. CORNELIUS helps JESUS up. LONGINIUS & LUCAS push JESUS to Altar.   SATANS distribute bottles to CENTURIONS & GUARDS.   GESTAS, laughing hysterically, points at JESUS. GUARD shoves GESTAS. DISMAS extends his hands, as if to help JESUS; GUARD beats DISMAS' hands.)

NARRATOR: Longinius and Lucas were forever ready to toast any occasion.

(LONGINIUS & LUCAS raise bottles, drink, toss bottles away. CORNELIUS pauses before consuming contents, tossing bottle away)

NARRATOR: Cornelius acknowledged that the hard drinking among Roman Guards helped them not to feel any pain from their conscience. *(CORNELIUS stares at LUCAS.)* Hard drinking helped them to become numb to the pain they inflicted.

(SATANS, with more bottles, approach GUARDs, salute GUARDS with bottles held high. SATANS drink bottles dry then toss them away.)

NARRATOR: From the corner of his eye, Cornelius saw Jesus' Mother, Mary. In shame Cornelius turned his face away from her.

(BOY SATAN gleefully approaches CORNELIUS & hands him a whip. SATAN GIRLS, with whips, pet LONGINIUS & LUCAS' arms & then hand them whips. GUARDS carry pillar, with ropes, to Altar)

NARRATOR: Cornelius heard the voices of the crowd shout to Pilate: "We have no king but Caesar! Crucify Jesus!" Cornelius mumbled to himself, "Why? What evil has Jesus done?" Longinius heard Cornelius' declaration; he then ordered Cornelius to be the first to strike Jesus. *(CORNELIUS, regrettably, strikes JESUS. SOUND EFFECT: WHIP)*

NARRATOR: Lucas and Longinius, as if in a tribal dance, began to strike Jesus over the head…upon the abdomen…shoulders…and back.

(SOUND EFFECT: WHIP. LONGINIUS & LUCAS strike JESUS. CORNELIUS reluctantly whips JESUS. MARY reaches towards JESUS. MARY MAGDALENE attempts to shield MARY. JOHN the APOSTLE hugs MARY. ANGELS bow & weep. SATANS, victoriously, raise their fists. PILATE approaches JESUS & GUARDS; raises his hand to stop the scourging. PILATE orders CORNELIUS to escort JESUS to Center.)

NARRATOR: Pilate shouted to the mob: "Look at the man! I find no guilt in him." But the crowd raucously cried: "FREE BARABBAS! CRUCIFY JESUS!"

(GESTAS gestures "thumbs-up!" DISMAS, shamefully, looks at ground. MR. SATAN, holding crown of thorns, "tip toes" to LUCAS. ANGELS weep. PILATE orders LUCAS to place crown of thorns on JESUS' head. LUCAS jams the crown of thorns into JESUS' skull. BOY & GIRL SATANS, hold red cloak. PILATE orders LONGINIUS & LUCAS to dress JESUS with cloak. LUCAS looks on ground, and retrieves Palm Branch. LUCAS approaches JESUS & hits JESUS over the head. LUCAS & LONGINIUS, mocking, bow before JESUS. LUCAS throws Palm Branch at JESUS.)

NARRATOR: Once more, Pilate presented Jesus to the crowd, saying: "Behold the Man!"

(MARY, crying, falls to her knees, placing her head into her palms. MARY MAGDALENE & JOHN the APOSTLE attempt to console MARY; ANGELS RAPHAEL & MICHAEL approach them & raise their arms in blessing.)

NARRATOR: Cornelius could not believe that the chief priests and the guards would lead the vicious chant: "CRUCIFY HIM, CRUCIFY HIM!" Pilate then screamed, "I find no case against this man. *(BOY & GIRL SATANS approach PILATE with water bowl; PILATE dips his fingers into bowl & shakes his fingers dry.)* Take him away and crucify him yourselves!"

(PONTIUS PILATE turns his back to the Audience and moves to Center. CLAUDIA slaps PILATE, then exits. MARY runs to JESUS. JOHN the APOSTLE follows MARY. LUCAS stops MARY; MARY slaps LUCAS. LONGINIUS orders LUCAS & CORNELIUS to push JESUS. JESUS, collapses to ground.)

NARRATOR: Like a volcano, anger spewed within Cornelius: he found it incredulous that Pontius Pilate, instead of doing what was right; cared more about what the public thought of him. Even though Cornelius was technically a pagan, he never believed that any action was right and moral, just because everyone else is doing it.

BLACKOUT

SCENE 12   JESUS BEARS HIS CROSS

(Lights still out. JESUS, bearing Cross, is between LONGINIUS (r) & CORNELIUS (l) at Center; LUCAS stands before JESUS. DISMAS, bearing cross, & GUARD at Altar   GESTAS, bearing cross, & GUARD at Center. TWO CHILDREN, carrying water bowls, ANGELS at left.   CONRAD & SATANS, with bottles, at right. MARY, MARY MAGDALENE, JOHN the APOSTLE & ANGEL GABRIEL at Center. Aisle.)

NARRATOR: *(During BLACKOUT)* As they prepared to take Jesus to Golgotha, known as the "Place of the Skull," Cornelius heard Pilate order Ethan the Crossmaker to make a sign with the inscription: "Jesus the Nazorean, the King of the Jews." Cornelius also heard Ethan grumble that Pontius Pilate always seemed to ruin his holiday with some last minute order! Cornelius did not particularly like Ethan...for he saw Ethan as an adult who never grew up. *(LIGHTS up. LONGINIUS, pushes JESUS forward.   SATANS, "falsely weeping," approach JESUS. CORNELIUS walks beside JESUS.   GESTAS & DISMAS move forward; GUARDS beat them. ANGELS gesture a "blessing" toward JESUS.)*

NARRATOR: Surrounding Cornelius were voices shouting, "JESUS DESERVES THIS!" Cornelius looked into the crowd and saw faces he knew from frequenting the local pubs; faces that were readily purchased for a flask of cheap ale. But, now, among the crowd, Cornelius saw a young, noble face whose mouth did not shout a word.

(CONRAD approaches GESTAS)

NARRATOR: Cornelius heard the young noble man say to Gestas, "I remember you! Years ago you tried to rob me!" *(GESTAS sneers at CONRAD.)* "It was near Bethlehem." *(GESTAS laughs)* Cornelius heard Gestas' cunning voice reply, "Still searching for another King?" *(GESTAS, mocking, nods his head toward JESUS)* "I have one for you— he's right behind me." *(GESTAS sadistically laughs)* He's the one with the crown of thorns." *(SATANS, clap. GUARD strikes GESTAS CONRAD looks at JESUS.)*

NARRATOR: Cornelius then heard Dismas say to Conrad, "Don't listen to Him; that's Jesus, he's..." *(GUARD strikes DISMAS LUCAS spits at CONRAD, ordering CONRAD to leave.)* Cornelius wondered who this brave young man was, and what Dismas was trying to tell him. *(LUCAS pushes CONRAD away. CONRAD draws his sword.)*

NARRATOR: Conrad was ready to defend his honor. But, just then, two young children came near. They were carrying bowls of water.

(CONRAD bows to the TWO YOUNG CHILDREN, then exits. LUCAS growls at CHILDREN; GESTAS "hisses" at children, GUARD strikes GESTAS; they move forward down aisle.)

NARRATOR: Seeing these youth, Cornelius became frightened for their safety. Immediately, he recalled the pleasure Longinius took in killing the Holy Innocents.

(TWO YOUNG CHILDREN kick LUCAS. DISMAS, tenderly, looks at CHILDREN. SATANS, approach CHILDREN. ANGELS, with outstretched hands, protect CHILDREN.)

NARRATOR: Nevertheless, Cornelius felt that these two youth had more courage than he; they tried to alleviate Jesus' pain by providing a sip of water.

(TWO YOUNG CHILDREN offer JESUS, water. JESUS gratefully, reaches out. LONGINIUS knocks water bowl from CHILDREN'S hands. LUCAS chases them away. ONE CHILD kicks LUCAS & ONE CHILD hits LUCAS, before they run off.)

Husbands, Wives; be open, listen to what the other is saying. Be willing to face the truth.

SCENE 13   ETHAN THE CROSSMAKER

NARRATOR: *(As LONGINIUS walks to ETHAN the CROSSMAKER)* Some thirty years ago, this Centurion started his military career with the slaughter of the Holy Innocents.   Somehow, in his pursuit to kill, he overlooked the manger where the angels protected   Mary, Joseph and the Infant Jesus. Somehow, he also overlooked Johanna and her infant child, Ethan, who were visiting the manger that night. Miraculously, their lives were spared.

(LUCAS leaves JESUS & GUARDS and walks behind LONGINIUS, slapping him on the back like a winning team-mate.)

NARRATOR: Now, with his son, Lucas, a mirror image of his father; they will concur in the murder of the Holy Innocents they missed those thirty years ago.

(LONGINIUS helps ETHAN the CROSSMAKER carry the Cross down aisle LUCAS, snickering, follows LONGINIUS. ETHAN the CROSSMAKER becomes horrified as he approaches JESUS.)

NARRATOR: Ethan the Crossmaker was a childhood friend of Jesus.

(ETHAN the CROSSMAKER drops the cross. JOHANNA, looking embarrassed, rushes to ETHAN.)

189

NARRATOR: Mary's husband, Joseph, taught the young Ethan and the young Jesus the art of woodworking.

(JOHNANNA rushes to MARY and tries to apologize)

NARRATOR: Ethan, the son of Johanna, was spared from murder, on that first   Christmas night. Ethan now realizes that he has made the instrument of death for his friend, Jesus.
(LONGINIUS and CORNELIUS pick up the cross and jam the cross onto JESUS' shoulders.)

NARRATOR: *(As ETHAN the CROSSMAKER begins to cry, placing his head into his hands.)* Parents have no control over what their children authentically become. *(JOHANNA follows ETHAN the CROSSMAKER, also crying)*

NARRATOR: Sometimes, we are all victims of circumstance.

(ETHAN the CROSSMAKER moves to JESUS, asking forgiveness. JOHANNA gives a "how could you" look to ETHAN, then intercedes, and asks JESUS for forgiveness. CAIAPHAS gloats.)

NARRATOR: Family members and friends sometimes have no idea how their actions will hurt others.

(JOHANNA goes toward MARY, asking forgiveness. MARY MAGDALENE and VERONICA slap ETHAN the CROSSMAKER'S face.)

NARRATOR: Mary Magdalene and Veronica lost their babies that first Christmas. They regret that Ethan's life was spared. *(JOHN the APOSTLE moves toward MARY MAGDALENE & VERONICA, trying to calm them. JUDAS looks at CAIAPHAS as if to say "I had no idea they were going to do this to Jesus!")*

NARRATOR: Our betrayals, at first innocent, have consequences that affect everyone and everything we know.

(LONGINIUS & CORNELIUS push JESUS, carrying cross, to left. As JESUS passes JUDAS, he pauses. JUDAS stares at JESUS. JESUS & CENTURIONS walk into the shadows.)

SCENE 14   JUDAS' DEATH

(JUDAS, holding a pouch containing silver coins, approaches CAIAPHAS. MR. SATAN holds a noose.)

NARRATOR: Once we welcome evil into our life, be prepared for its consequences.

(JUDAS throws money back at CAIAPHAS who laughs and exits. Mr. SATAN hands JUDAS the noose.)

NARRATOR: Evil knows no boundaries; evil will get rid of evil to achieve its goals. *(JUDAS makes a pleading motion to Audience as he faces the noose.)*

NARRATOR: As a human being, how do we forgive ourselves for grave mistakes we make? What do we not forgive ourselves for? Or, like Judas, do we mistakenly believe we cannot be forgiven? *(BOY SATAN approaches JUDAS.)* It is thought that Judas could not forgive himself for having been abused as a child, *(BOY SATAN pokes JUDAS.)* or that Judas, himself was a child abuser. *(GIRL SATAN moves toward JUDAS, taking his hand, petting it, then giving the "loser" sign at JUDAS. SATANS exit)*

NARRATOR: Judas would not allow the Light of Christ to touch his pain.

(Frightened, JUDAS walks down Aisle, pleading with Audience. Then JUDAS holds up noose and stares at it with "crazed" look.)

BLACKOUT

NARRATOR: *(During BLACKOUT)* As family members, we tailor-fit our own nooses, when we fail to give our pain, our darkness to God. Those deadly times we refuse to forgive ourselves and one another.

SCENE 15   PILATE'S DEMISE

(Lights still out. PONTIUS PILATE & CLAUDIA, PILATE'S WIFE at Center)

NARRATOR: Evil achieves its own domino effect. *(LIGHTS UP)* Pilate's wife was truly alone, even while her husband was alive. Loneliness, with its feelings of anger and failure, intensifies when we fail to acknowledge one another under our very own roofs. *(PONTIUS PILATE waves his hand in disgust at CLAUDIA, as he walks to front.)*

NARRATOR: It is thought that Pontius Pilate took his own life for fear of the mess he made of his career. *(PONTIUS PILATE pulls out noose and walks down Aisle, interacting with Audience)* the mess he made of his family, the mess he made of himself.

(SATANS enter from left and applaud.)

NARRATOR: Moment by moment, word by lack of word, we hang ourselves whenever we do not admit our faults. If only Pilate owned up to his failures rather than trying to get ahead in spite of them.

BLACKOUT

NARRATOR: *(During BLACKOUT)* Weakness desires to bring others down.

SCENE 16   THE GOOD & BAD THIEVES

(Lights are still out. DISMAS, the Good Thief, holding cross, GUARD, ANGELS at left. GESTAS, the Bad Thief, holding cross, GUARD, SATANS, CAIAPHAS at right)

NARRATOR: *(During BLACKOUT)* On Good Friday, Two Thieves were to be crucified with Jesus. One can't help wonder what their family life was like; Did they have one? Was it lacking? Or was it like a Norman Rockwell Family Portrait? Even if it was, there are no guarantees.

(LIGHTS UP. DISMAS at left front & GESTAS at right front.)

NARRATOR: Sometimes the best of families produce good as well as evil. Could these two Thieves, DISMAS and GESTAS, *(DISMAS & GESTAS, carrying crosses, move to Center. GUARDS, ANGELS & SATANS accompany respective THIEVES.)* have been like the Prodigal Son and his brother? Remember, the Prodigal Son's older brother freely chose the evil of jealousy, of being resentful of his father's generosity toward his younger brother. The older brother is like GESTAS, the Bad Thief.

(GESTAS snarls at Audience, spits at his GUARD.)

NARRATOR: GESTAS revolted against everyone and everything. He refused to see any goodness in life

(CAIAPHAS enters from right front laughing at GESTAS, who spits at CAIAPHAS. CAIAPHAS spits back at GESTAS.).

NARRATOR: While being crucified, GESTAS cursed, mocked Jesus in demanding that   Jesus perform a miracle. Legend states that GESTAS, while hanging on his cross, had his eyes plucked out by a crow. Like GESTAS, does our anger blind us to the conversion that is possible? *(GESTAS proudly beats his chest.)*

NARRATOR: GESTAS never believed that his life could be transformed. His only belief was in the Evil of ultimate selfishness.

(GUARD pushes GESTAS to ground. The cross also falls to ground. GUARD then steps   on GESTAS. CAIAPHAS and SATANS laugh and spit at GESTAS.)

NARRATOR: Could it be that DISMAS met Jesus...while the infant Jesus lay on the hay, in the manger, that first Christmas Night?

(DISMAS is pushed to Front by GUARD.   ANGELS open their wings. GESTAS rises, spits at DISMAS. GUARDS separate them.)

NARRATOR: DISMAS had no one, in his life, to show him what is good and true, something he always desired, especially so. With eyes open wide, DISMAS saw three Wise Men come to the manger, placing before the Infant Jesus gifts of gold, frankincense and myrrh.

(DISMAS, shamefully, bows his head.)

NARRATOR: That night, all DISMAS had to offer Jesus was the gift of music on his drum. Yes, today, Good Friday, DISMAS, the Drummer Boy. a Prodigal Son, encounters Jesus, once again. *(DISMAS falls to his knees, begins to cry, then folds his hands in prayer.)*

NARRATOR: Years ago, with love, *(GUARD strikes DISMAS across the back)*, DISMAS reached out to the Infant Jesus, with music on his drum.

Today, on the cross, DISMAS once again reaches out to Jesus. Only this time he asks for a gift-- instead of giving one...DISMAS wishes to know the music of redeeming love. In turn, DISMAS receives the gift of Paradise. *(DISMAS rises)* A Prodigal Son reunited with the love and forgiveness of God the Father. *(ANGELS reach towards DISMAS.)*

BLACKOUT

SCENE 17   JESUS BEARS HIS CROSS / FALL

(Lights still out. JESUS bearing Cross, LONGINIUS, CORNELIUS, LUCAS at Center R, Two WATER BOYS at Center L.)

NARRATOR: As Jesus' hands embraced the Wood of the Cross, *(LIGHTS UP)* He must have recalled *(JESUS begins down aisle)* the numerous times His hands embraced wood in Joseph's carpentry shop; a loving, free embrace. Now, Jesus, the carpenter's Son, applies His artistry to a final masterpiece with wood. In His youth, with Joseph, Jesus gave shape to the wood. Today, on the way to Calvary, the wood will whittle Him.

(Two WATER BOYS offer JESUS water. LUCAS knocks the water from their hands. LONGINIUS scares the WATER BOYS away. LUCAS strikes JESUS. JESUS falls to ground with cross falling on his back. LUCAS kicks at JESUS. LONGINIUS tries to stop LUCAS from kicking JESUS.)

SCENE 18   MARY

(JOHN the APOSTLE enters, & runs to help JESUS. MARY, MARY MAGDALENE & ANGELS follow JOHN the APOSTLE. ETHAN the CROSSMAKER & JOHANNA enter left. SATANS enter right. JOHN the APOSTLE reaches to help JESUS. LUCAS pushes him away. MARY, with outstretched arms, goes to JESUS.)

NARRATOR: What was on Mary's mind that day? Seeing Her Son led to execution on a cross made by Jesus' friend.

(ETHAN the CROSSMAKER approaches MARY to offer comfort. MARY studies his face, then turns away. ETHAN remains in place, as if frozen.)

NARRATOR: How many parents are ashamed of the occupations of their children?

(JOHANNA approaches her son, ETHAN, and tries to escort   ETHAN away from MARY.   JOHANNA's eyes remain fixed on MARY as if to say "I'm sorry")

NARRATOR: Mary knew that Johanna's heart was breaking—just like her own heart.   Mothers know the hearts of their children.

(ETHAN the CROSSMAKER goes to help JESUS.   GESTAS & SATANS & GUARDS point & laugh as ETHAN goes to JESUS. LUCAS pushes ETHAN to the ground. JESUS stares into the eyes of ETHAN.   GUARDS force JESUS & ETHAN to their feet. LUCAS strikes ETHAN.   JOHANNA runs to help ETHAN & JESUS but GUARDS shove her away. LONGINIUS & CORNELIUS place cross on JESUS' shoulders. MARY goes to help JOHANNA.)

NARRATOR: Yet, as parents must, Mary had the tough love, the courage needed, to intervene when her child's life was in the wrongful hands of others.

.

(LUCAS pushes ETHAN into JOHANNA. MARY stares at ETHAN & JOHANNA who then exit. MARY places her hands atop JESUS' hands. And walks with JESUS down the Aisle. ANGELS bow toward MARY & JESUS. GUARDS, GESTAS, SATANS mock.)

NARRATOR: We often remove ourselves from painful decisions which require our "tough love." Or, we stay in hurtful situations. Like Mary, are we fearless as we act on the love we feel?

(MARY & JESUS walk to Front. GUARDS approach them. LUCAS raises his sword. MARY stares at GUARDS & LUCAS; holds out her hand, warning: "back off." MARY soothes JESUS' forehead along the crown of thorns. LUCAS raises his sword to strike MARY. JOHN the APOSTLE & MARY MAGDALENE help MARY to move back. MARY reaches towards JESUS, and JESUS reaches out to MARY. JOHANNA goes to JESUS.)

NARRATOR: We need not apologize for the lives of our adult children. We allow them to rise or fall by themselves, we love them, even when we do not love their actions.

(CAIAPHAS GUARDS, SATANS, GESTAS mock JOHANNA. SATANS prompt GUARDS to push JESUS into Center Aisle. JESUS falls to ground with cross. JOHANNA backs away. Wanting to help her son, MARY runs to JESUS but is held back by JOHN the APOSTLE & MARY MAGDALENE. MARY'S hands reach out to JESUS through the arms of JOHN the APOSTLE and MARY MAGDALENE.)

NARRATOR: Yes, to love our children, even when we are powerless to help them, then, to accept and love ourselves when we want to help but are prevented from doing so by forces beyond our power. (JOHN the APOSTLE & MARY MAGDALENE hug MARY; pulling MARY back.)

SCENE 19   SIMON OF CYRENE

(SIMON of CYRENE, holding basket of eggs, at Center. CORNELIUS starts down aisle scouting the Audience)

NARRATOR: Family members often pull us into unwelcome situations like Simon of Cyrene *(SIMON of CYRENE starts down aisle)* Who was chosen to help Jesus carry His Cross.

(GUARDS "back-kick" Simon who tries to protect egg basket LUCAS takes egg basket & plays with eggs)

NARRATOR: Simon was not one of the famous twelve apostles. Yet, nonetheless, he was a follower of Jesus. *(LUCAS puts basket down)* Simon of Cyrene was in town to sell his prized eggs at market. *(CORNELIUS pushes SIMON to ground. LUCAS raises SIMON up. LONGINIUS & GUARDS raise JESUS to his feet and place cross on His shoulder. JESUS nearly collapses to his knees. LONGINIUS signals CORNELIUS & LUCAS to transfer the cross from JESUS' shoulder to SIMON'S shoulder.)*

NARRATOR: Sometimes, God answers our prayers through the help of others. Sometimes, it is necessary that we let go of our crosses just as Jesus did. Mysteriously, God answers our prayers by making us face the things we wanted to let go of.

(LONGINIUS shoves JESUS down aisle. CORNELIUS directs SIMON to follow JESUS. LUCAS pushes SIMON. As JESUS & SIMON reach Front, DISMAS breaks free from GUARD, drops cross, and reaches out to JESUS. GESTAS drops cross and tries to attack DISMAS. GUARDS recapture DISMAS & GESTAS, forcing them back to their crosses. CAIAPHAS "Air-fiddles." Remaining CAST reacts.)

BLACKOUT

SCENE 20   VERONICA

NARRATOR: Veronica has never forgotten the day Jesus healed her hemorrhaging. *(VERONICA at center)*

(LIGHTS UP. VERONICA starts down aisle)

NARRATOR: Veronica also recalled the brutal spilling of her infant's blood on the night the Holy Innocents were murdered. Now, Veronica wishes to end another hemorrhaging, that of Jesus' Blood.

(As VERONICA approaches JESUS, MR. SATAN hands CAIAPHAS, rose petals. CAIAPHAS, in mock sympathy, throws rose petals on VERONICA as she walks by him. ANGELS bow to VERONICA)

NARRATOR: *(As VERONICA nears JESUS)* In the guise of goodness, fear tries to stop the good that may be done.
(JOHANNA enters from left, trying to stop VERONICA. ETHAN the CROSSMAKER enters to retrieve JOHANNA. VERONICA approaches JESUS, removes her veil & wipes JESUS' face. CAIAPHAS mocks VERONICA. DISMAS reaches toward JESUS. GESTAS pretends to vomit. SATANS pretend to "choke." LONGINIUS signals VERONICA back with his spear.)

NARRATOR: Like Veronica, we can become human angels to each other. *(ANGELS "angel flake" VERONICA as she wipes JESUS' face)*

NARRATOR: Ties of loving gratitude are often thicker than ties of blood. *(VERONICA leaves JESUS. SATANS incite CAIAPHAS to "do something!" CAIAPHAS sticks out his foot to trip VERONICA; she falls face down into her veil. VERONICA rises, wipes her face with her veil, unaware that the imprint of JESUS' face is on the veil facing the Audience VERONICA walks away.)*

SCENE   21   FALL OF THE THIEVES

(As VERONICA exits, GUARD, clubs GESTAS, and GESTAS' cross falls to ground. GESTAS also falls. GUARD drags GESTAS back to his cross.

SATANS rub their hands in glee. GUARD strikes DISMAS. GUARDS then place crosses on JESUS & SIMON'S shoulders.)

NARRATOR: As God's Family, we all carry Crosses: an illness, perhaps an emotional condition or breakdown; the Cross of Dreams never attained. Yet, the worst Cross of all: the failure to truly love.

BLACKOUT

SCENE 22   WOMEN OF JERUSALEM

(Lights still out. WOMAN, holding baby, 2nd WOMAN, holding baby, with TWO YOUNG CHILDREN at Center. MOTHER of the GOOD THIEF & TIRA, JOHNANNA, ETHAN the CROSSMAKER at left, MOTHER of BAD THIEF at right)

NARRATOR: *(During BLACKOUT.)* Some of the Women of Jerusalem were Mothers of the Holy Innocents. Yes, they endured the shocking loss of a child, but they also were open to whatever future Blessings God and His Angels would deliver.

(LIGHTS UP. WOMAN holding baby walks down Center Aisle)

NARRATOR: Yes, second chances—like the time Jesus met this Samaritan Woman at Jacob's Well.

(WOMAN approaches JESUS. GESTAS tries to push her back. WOMAN slaps GESTAS. SATANS give a "thumbs-up.")

NARRATOR: This woman had multiple failed marriages. Jesus knew her need to be understood, forgiven, and valued; the Blessing of True Love.

(MOTHER of the GOOD THIEF enters. SIMON of CYRENE removes cross from JESUS' shoulder)

NARRATOR: Some children grow up to be disappointments to their parents. *(MOTHER of GOOD THIEF scolds DISMAS.)*

NARRATOR: Some parents grow up to be disappointments to their children. DISMAS' mother was an absentee parent. She heard that DISMAS was in Jerusalem that day. She brings her pain to Jesus. *(MOTHER of the BAD THIEF enters)*

NARRATOR: For all children have possibilities to achieve dreams, as well as the possibilities for Good as well as for Evil. So do their parents.

(MOTHER of the BAD THIEF goes to GESTAS, gesturing "show me the money!")

NARRATOR: Usually, a child's choice for a path of good, or a path of evil; is steered by decisions made by parents' decisions, which leave a lasting impression. *(GESTAS spits at his mother)*

NARRATOR: GESTAS' Mother introduced him to a life of crime from an early age; small items: an apple, or grape at market. Larger items as he grew older. She sold him into slavery for a bottle. She heard he was in town this Good Friday. Why not one last shake-down? Children return the love, respect; or lack of love, lack of respect, that they were shown.

(SATANS tempt MOTHER of the BAD THIEF; she cries.)

NARRATOR: Wrongly, parents often believe that it is too late for their children; or for themselves; to improve.

(2nd WOMAN, holding baby, & TWO YOUNG CHILDREN walks down Aisle.)

NARRATOR: For a brief moment, these women, their children, meet Ultimate Goodness; Ultimate Love in Jesus.

(ANGELS bow to 2nd WOMAN, holding baby, & TWO YOUNG CHILDREN. GESTAS & SATANS try to stop WOMAN from moving toward JESUS. Yet, WOMAN & TWO YOUNG CHILDREN walk past them.)

NARRATOR: ...even though Ultimate Evil knocked at their door.

(SATANS command LONGINIUS, CORNELIUS, LUCAS & GUARDS to remove the WOMEN. BOY SATAN & GIRL SATAN approach the TWO YOUNG CHILDREN. ANGELS raise their wings protecting the TWO YOUNG CHILDREN. LONGINIS orders CORNELIUS, LUCAS & GUARDS to pull the WOMEN away from JESUS.)

NARRATOR: The Roman Guards had no respect for women or for children. Whose Life have we no Respect for?

(TIRA enters at left. DISMAS, surprised, watches TIRA closely. LONGINIUS stares at her. TIRA runs to help the 2nd WOMAN, holding baby, & TWO YOUNG CHILDREN. LUCAS tries to stop TIRA from helping WOMAN & TWO CHILDREN. TIRA slaps LUCAS.)

NARRATOR: Some parents, stay at the sidelines of their Family's Life.

(ETHAN the CROSSMAKER, looking perplexed, enters, looking for the WOMAN & her TWO YOUNG CHILDREN. JOHANNA enters & slaps ETHAN.)

NARRATOR: Yes, Parents, ashamed for their adult

children's lack of attention, lack of protection for their spouses and children; is often behavior their children learned from them.

(JOHANNA enters Center; she begins to plead with Audience.)

NARRATOR: Like Johanna, ashamed, that while Ethan was young, she could have given him more attention, more love; introduced him to more faith. She knew she should have been more grateful for the Blessing of Ethan's life being spared thirty years ago. Yet, like Johanna, once we get what we want from God; we forget God; until days like this.

(LUCAS, dazed by TIRA's slap, joins CORNELIUS & GUARDS who continue to push WOMEN & CHILDREN away. SATANS raise staffs in glee. DISMAS looks at scene with sadness. GESTAS shows great anger. JESUS reaches out to the WOMEN & CHILDREN.)

NARRATOR: In varied ways, Jesus reached out and touched the hearts and souls of these women. His example empowers us to never underestimate our ability to reach out, if only to touch.

(GUARDS beat DISMAS & GESTAS. DISMAS reaches out to his MOTHER & again is struck by the GUARD. LONGINIUS orders CORNELIUS to beat SIMON of CYRENE & JESUS. LONGINIUS orders SIMON of CYRENE & JESUS to, again, carry the cross.)

SCENE 23   JESUS' GREAT FALL

NARRATOR: Yes, at times, even the best of families can be like roses: out of any beauty, only the thorns remain. They slowly move into the center aisle. LUCAS continues to beat Simon. *(SIMON displays anger toward LUCAS, who strikes JESUS. JESUS collapses, in spectacular fashion, with cross catapulting into Aisle.)*

NARRATOR: Family Members sometimes smile when relatives, ex-spouses, brothers, sisters, favored son or daughter crash and burn; especially when the pedestal was tall. *(SIMON of CYRENE, enraged, fights with GUARDS. ANGELS & SATANS draw near.)*

NARRATOR: A fall from grace, from the seemingly perfect marriage, from the apparently wonderful job, the foreclosure of a house, repossession of a car, the filing for bankruptcy, the fall from dignity, popularity or fame. When we fall the hardest, good and evil pull at us the hardest.

(SIMON of CYRENE reaches down to assist JESUS, lying—as if dead—on the ground. As SIMON does so, SATANS grab SIMON'S left arm. Next, ANGELS grab SIMON'S right arm; as if SIMON were in the middle of a tug-of-war. LUCAS brutally clubs SIMON. SIMON, as if dead, falls,)

BLACKOUT

SCENE 24   STRIPPING OF JESUS' GARMENTS

(Lights are still out. JESUS' Cross is placed on floor in Front of altar; the cross stand is placed at Center. Crosses for DISMAS & GESTAS are placed into their stands at right & left. JESUS, LONGINIUS, CORNELIUS, LUCAS, with dice, at Center. GESTAS, GUARD, holding rope, SATANS & CAIAPHAS at right. DISMAS, GUARD, holding rope, ANGELS at left. MARY, MARY MAGDALENE, VERONICA & JOHN the APOSTLE are at foot of JESUS' Cross. SIMON of CYRENE stands to their right & JOHANNA, ETHAN the CROSSMAKER stand to their left. TWO YOUNG CHILDREN at Center Aisle Back Remaining CAST stands in Front of altar.)

NARRATOR: *(During BLACKOUT)* There are good strippings, and there are bad strippings in our lives.

NARRATOR: The Good Thief, DISMAS, *(LIGHTS UP)* though stripped of his garments, that day, became a Disciple of Jesus.

(GUARD tears off DISMAS' garments, then ropes DISMAS to the cross.)

NARRATOR: DISMAS desired to clothe himself with the prayer of trust; the trust he would have a share in JESUS' Heavenly Kingdom; unlike Judas whose sole interest was in an Earthly Kingdom. DISMAS is the patron saint for any family member who may have to deal with a death sentence.

(DISMAS looks prayerfully upward. GUARD snickers.)

NARRATOR: The Bad Thief GESTAS, continued to strip himself of any goodness.

(GUARD tears off GESTAS' garments. GESTAS proudly exhibits his physique. GUARD slaps GESTAS & begins to rope GESTAS to the cross.)

NARRATOR: Mocking JESUS, GESTAS demanded a miracle. Sadly, He represents those family members who don't have logical reasons for rejecting any love, any goodness that is present. *(GESTAS, gleefully, spits at GUARD.)*

NARRATOR: As Jesus was stripped of His garments...

(LONGINOUS orders LUCAS & CORNELIUS to strip JESUS. They toss JESUS' garment into the air. When garment falls on the ground, they throw dice, gambling for it. LUCAS wins, raising garment in victory!)

NARRATOR: Jesus' heart joins that of every parent whose heart and soul know the words Jesus spoke: "Blessed are you when they insult you, and persecute you, and utter every kind of evil falsely, against you, because of me."

(CORNELIUS shoves JESUS, then throws Him to the ground. MARY reaches out to JESUS. JOHANNA hits ETHAN as she points her finger towards MARY & JESUS.)

NARRATOR: Parents, at any age, are never too old to let their children know what they truly think of them.

(LONGINIUS, CORNELIUS & LUCAS stretch JESUS' body upon the cross. MARY MAGDALENE, VERONICA & JOHN the APOSTLE reach towards JESUS. TWO YOUNG CHILDREN run down Center Aisle to MARY. LUCAS, laughing, flaunts JESUS' garment & dice into MARY'S face.)

BLACKOUT

(Lights still out. LONGINIUS, CORNELIUS, & LUCAS, holding hammers high, each kneel, on one knee, by JESUS' hands and feet.)

NARRATOR: *(During BLACKOUT)* Unfortunately, good family members allow themselves to be corrupted. They give in to values, practices, and habits that are shameful. These actions kill others, even though it is not by their own hand. *(Lights are still out. LONGINIUS, at JESUS' left arm, CORNELIUS at JESUS' right arm, LUCAS at JESUS' feet; raise hammers high.)*

SCENE 25   NAILING

(Lights still out. CAIAPHAS & SATAN FAMILY behind altar: GIRL SATAN holds Sign, remaining Satan Family Members each hold Nail. ANGELS, MARY, MARY MAGDALENE, JOHN the APOSTLE, & VERONICA to Left of Cross. Rest of CAST hold in place. LIGHTS UP. SATANS look at Nails they hold. CAIAPHAS, impatient, grabs nails from SATANS and distributes

Nails to LONGINIUS, CORNELIUS & LUCAS, who place Nails into JESUS'
hands and feet, then raise their hammers high. ETHAN runs to CAIAPHAS
and then to LONGINIUS)

VOICE of ETHAN the CROSSMAKER: They never used nails to
crucify criminals on my crosses before!   WHY are you using NAILS
TODAY!? Why aren't you using ropes?" (CAIAPHAS belly-laughs and
snorts like a pig)

NARRATOR: Lucas, the Younger Centurion, only wanted to get the
job done, and go home to celebrate the holiday. With time, Lucas
became desensitized to killing.

(LUCAS shoves ETHAN, raises his hammer & strikes ETHAN. ETHAN falls.
JOHANNA cries aloud. MARY rushes to ETHAN, places her hands over him
as if in Blessing.)

NARRATOR: Despite a Mother's own pain, a Mother always reaches
out to help, to heal. (ETHAN rises. JOHANNA embraces ETHAN. JOHN
the APOSTLE embraces MARY.)

NARRATOR: Never underestimate the intercession of a loving Mother.
Many miracles, not recorded in Scripture, also came from Mary's love
that day.
                              BLACKOUT

NARRATOR: (During BLACKOUT) There is a prayer called: "The Silent
Prayer of Nailing." Whenever we are in a situation beyond our control,
simply open the palms of our hands, exposing ourselves to whatever is
about to happen, and trust in God's providential care.

(SOUND EFFECTS: Hammering/Nailing. After10 to 12 hammer strikes:
LIGHTS UP. LONGINIUS, CORNELIUS, LUCAS continue to Nail JESUS to

Cross. JESUS, in violent pain, writhes. MARY, near fainting, reaches out to JESUS. CAIAPHAS, laughing, pushes MARY back. JOHN the APOSTLE & MARY MAGDALENE assist MARY. CAIAPHAS confiscates sign from GIRL SATAN & hands Sign to LONGINIUS. In puzzlement, LONGINIUS reads Sign, questioning its inscription. LUCAS snatches Sign from LONGINIUS & nails Sign to top of Cross. MARY cries aloud. MRS. SATAN, in menaces MARY.)

NARRATOR: The sign placed, on Jesus' Cross, mocked Jesus with the title: "He Claimed to Be King of the Jews." *(MRS. SATAN mocks MARY'S tears.)*

NARRATOR: What mocking do we hammer upon family; upon friends?

BLACKOUT

(Lights still out. Cross set in stand at Top Center. JESUS crucified on Cross, His hands are also roped to Cross. JESUS is between LONGINIUS, holding spear & CORNELIUS. Nearby, is SIMON of CYRENE., MARY, MARY AGDALENE, JOHN the APOSTLE & VERONICA. ANGELS place their hands upon their shoulders. Nearby is JOHANNA & ETHAN. GESTAS' Cross placed in stand at Right. GESTAS crucified /roped to Cross. GUARDS, CAIAPHAS & SATANS stand close. DISMAS' Cross in stand at Left. DISMAS stands crucified. GUARDS stand near him. WOMEN of JERUSALEM, YOUNG CHILDREN, CAST are kneeling and grieving: some, refusing to look, have their heads buried in their hands.)

(SOUND EFFECTS: THUNDER, LIGHTNING, CREEPY LAUGHTER)

NARRATOR: *(During BLACKOUT & when CAST in place)* The true test of the Cross; of the Crosses we all carry; is the painful process of saying the unexpected, yet, wanted, goodbyes. The goodbyes that are shocking horrifying words to those who eternally love. But, is it really goodbye? Or is it a welcome?

(LIGHTS UP)

SCENE 26   CRUCIFIXION

(JESUS, looking up, breathes heavily. His chest heaves, His stomach collapses. JESUS' entire body writhes in shock) SOUND EFFECTS: THUNDER, LIGHTNING)

VOICE of JESUS: "Forgive them Father, for they don't know what they are doing." *(Long Pause)* "I thirst." *(LONGINIUS, places sponge on tip of spear, raises it to JESUS' lips. JESUS refuses)*

VOICE of JESUS: "My God, My God! Why? Have You abandoned Me?" *(LONGINIUS, removing sponge from spear, and readies spear to strike. JOHANNA goes to LONGINIUS.)*

NARRATOR: Johanna knew that there was something familiar about the Centurion. She definitely recognized him. *(JOHANNA grabs LONGINIUS' spear, daring to hold it still.)*

NARRATOR: Johanna shouted.

VOICE OF JOHANNA: "You're the One! Thirty years ago, I met you in Bethlehem at the Innkeeper's Manger! You may not remember, but, you spared Jesus' life. He was the Infant born in the manger; and I was there, too, with my Infant son, Ethan, your Crossmaker! The Angels protected us! You looked at all of us as if you didn't see us. You can't take Jesus' life today! Please!! Please!!" *(JOHANNA falls upon her knees)*

VOICE of JESUS: "Father, it is Finished. Into Your Hands, I place my Spirit."

(LONGINIUS, regains composure, raises his spear, pauses, looks at JOHANNA, then looks upon JESUS. LUCAS, angrily, approaches LONGINIUS who hands his spear to LUCAS.)

NARRATOR: Some of us are propelled into the horrible choice of maintaining life, or ending it.

(LUCAS, stepping back, readies his spear to pierce JESUS. LONGINIUS nods "Yes." As LUCAS steps forward, JOHANNA steps in front of LUCAS.)

VOICE OF JOHANNA: "NO!"

NARRATOR: Unfairly, life horribly drops us. We are forced to make decisions where no one can win. *(LUCAS hands the spear back to LONGINIUS)*

NARRATOR: Like Lucas, the Centurion, sometimes we have to give up, and give back. Yet, our jobs, our families, friends create situations where we should NOT go.

(LONGINIUS, with hand shaking, goes into a rage & taunts CAST. As if crazed, LONGINIUS threatens Audience with his Spear. Then, like a knight in a Jousting Tournament, he charges and plunges Spear into JESUS. MARY rushes to JESUS, bends down and hugs His' feet. LONGINIUS drops Spear. SATANS hand a Spear to GESTAS' GUARD who impales GESTAS and breaks GESTAS' bones. CAST responds. LONGINIUS orders CORNELIUS & LUCAS to remove the Nails from JESUS' body.)

BLACKOUT

NARRATOR: *(During BLACKOUT)* When love is authentic, we desire what is best for our loved ones. Can we, with tearful joy, give them back to God?   Back to the God, who lovingly loaned them to us; even if only for a short while?

MUSIC INTERLUDE

(Lights still out. MARY sits, holding JESUS' dead body in her arms; JOHN the APOSTLE, MARY MAGDALENE & VERONICA, holding herbs SIMON of CYRENE, holding Sign, stands behind JOHN the APOSTLE. ETHAN & JOHANNA, holding burial cloth, at Left. ANGELS form "arch" around MARY & JESUS. DISMAS & GESTAS remain on their Crosses. GUARDS, holding Burial Cloths stand near. TIRA & Remaining CAST are grieving. WOMEN hold flowers. JESUS' Cross remains in stand at Center until the end of play.)

SCENE 27: REMOVAL FROM CROSS AND BURIAL

NARRATOR: (During BLACKOUT) ETHAN, the Crossmaker, made countless crosses; instruments of torture for Rome's criminals. Today is different; it is the first time Ethan will provide an instrument of comfort.

LIGHTS UP

(MARY removes Crown of Thorns from JESUS' head. SIMON of CYRENE, angrily looks at Sign & throws it aside. ETHAN & JOHANNA, bring the burial cloth to Mary. ANGELS assist ETHAN & JOHANNA in placing Burial Cloth over JESUS' body. TWO CHILDREN hug MARY. ANGELS bow & SATANS jeer. VERONICA lifts Burial Cloth, and sprinkles herbs on JESUS' body.)

NARRATOR: Veronica's Veil comforted Jesus' painful face. Now, Veronica covers Jesus' Body with herbs, according to Jewish practice. (MARY MAGDALENE attempts to stop VERONICA, wanting to share the anointing of the Body, JOHN the APOSTLE gently intervenes. MARY looks upon them sadly)
NARRATOR: Often times, at Funerals, families argue over who does what; or gets what. As the Old Testament reminds us, there is a right

time and a right place for everything. Do not disrespect the dead with such self-centered, insensitive behavior. *(GUARDS cut ropes on DISMAS & GESTAS' crosses: DISMAS & GESTAS' bodies fall to ground. GUARDS, laughing, throw Burial Cloths on DISMAS & GESTAS' bodies. Laughing. SATANS poke dead THIEVES' bodies.)*

NARRATOR: On their own, skeletons come out of closets at Funerals. Today, is one such day for DISMAS the Good Thief. his mother, Tira, was present for his funeral. today.

(TIRA, holding flower, approaches DISMAS' body.)

NARRATOR: TIRA is also the mother of young Lucas, the Assistant Centurion. She had never married his father, LONGINIUS.

(As TIRA is about to place flower, LUCAS tries to stop her. TIRA slaps LUCAS.)

VOICE of TIRA: Don't you dare slap your mother!

VOICE of LUCAS: "Woman, Don't lie to me! My old man told me that my mother died years ago!" *(LONGINIUS "arm-locks" LUCAS. SATANS snicker).*

VOICE of LONGINIUS: Lucas, I've made too many mistakes throughout my life. I even had to kill an innocent man today! Please, please don't become what I am. Start over your life. It's not too late!

(LUCAS spits at LONGINIUS, jeers at MARY, then exits angrily through the Audience. TIRA slaps LONGINIUS and exits. LONGINIUS, stoically, remains in place.)

NARRATOR: It is never too late, for any of us. Life hands us thousands of chances to start again, all we have to do is choose one. *(ANGELS form "Honor Guard" behind MARY & JESUS. WOMEN & CHILDREN place flowers on JESUS' Body. As flowers are placed, SATANS regurgitate. WOMEN & CHILDREN exit. After final flower is placed, SATANS spit at JESUS' body and exit, laughing. Upon SATANS' exit, JOHN the APOSTLE places his arm on MARY'S shoulder.)*

NARRATOR: From that day, onward, John did as Jesus wished. He took Mary into His care as His own Mother.

(SIMON of CYRENE steps forward to pay respect to MARY & JESUS. SIMON exits, searching for his egg basket.)

NARRATOR: What beauty can we return for the beauty of loving family members? It is thought that Simon went on to become a disciple. Here, he searches for the basket of eggs that he lost, wondering if any would be intact to eat. *(SIMON of CYRENE finds egg basket)*

NARRATOR: But, to Simon's surprise, he finds a delightful feast-- of intact eggs-- gloriously colored! Thus, the tradition of coloring Eggs for Easter is born. *(SIMON of CYRENE shows Audience the colored eggs as he exits).*

NARRATOR: Yet, love, and beauty are not recognized by everyone – they threaten those whose purpose is to degrade.

(GUARDS approach MARY. They snicker & irreverently exit-as team mates. CORNELIUS, unable to look at MARY, stoically exits)

NARRATOR: No one is beyond redemption, regardless of whatever we may have done.

(LONGINIUS comes forward, bows & removes Helmet)

NARRATOR: As Jesus' life and teachings remind us-- all we need is to love--and to live out that love with our neighbor—as well as our self.

(MARY, with a forgiving look, nods to LONGINIUS, who stares at MARY, then exits, with head bowed. MARY MAGDALENE & VERONICA hug MARY, then exit. JOHN the APOSTLE, holding two flowers, prompts MARY to leave. MARY rises; she and JOHN stare at JESUS' covered body. JOHN places flower on JESUS' body, then hands MARY a flower. MARY kisses her flower—raises flower to Heaven—ANGELS raise high their "wings" MARY drops flower upon JESUS' covered body. JOHN supports MARY as they exit. ANGELS remain as "guards" around JESUS' body. CAIAPHAS "sneaks out" & gleefully "examines" JESUS' lifeless body, then laughs as he proclaims...)

VOICE of CAIAPHAS: "HE'S DEAD!" *(CAIAPHAS, laughing, exits. As CAIAPHAS leaves. LIGHTS OUT.)*

MUSICAL INTERLUDE   BLACKOUT

<u>SCENE 28</u>   FINDING   AN   EMPTY   TOMB

(Lights are still out. JESUS, JOHANNA & ETHAN at Center, ANGEL GABRIEL is between ANGELS MICHAEL and RAPHAEL. JOHN the APOSTLE at Right, MARY MAGDALENE at Left THIEVES' BODIES, Crosses & Stands are removed.)

NARRATOR: Family Members who become caretakers experience the pain of a different sort of burial...the burial of a free schedule, the grave of an un-peaceful mind and fearful heart. The death of a life we once knew...yet, because of selfless, loving care—caretakers also experience the promise of a rising to new life. What tombs are our lives currently in? *(LIGHTS UP, MARY MAGDALENE & JOHN the APOSTLE cautiously approach ANGEL GABRIEL.)*

NARRATOR: "He is not here!" were the words the Angel Gabriel told Mary Magdalene and John. Do we really believe in the promise of eternal life today, by living as if there weren't one?

BLACKOUT

SCENE 29   RESURRECTION

(Lights are still out. MARY at Center; CAST remains in place. JESUS' Burial Cloth is draped upon the crossbeam of JESUS' Cross which remains in Stand at Center.)

MUSIC: HANDEL'S HALLELUIAH CHORUS

(On the third "Alleluia:" LIGHTS UP. JESUS comes down Center Aisle. MARY MAGDALENE, enters from Left. Simultaneously, MARY runs into Main Aisle & greets JESUS. MARY MAGDALENE stops to Altar; Together, JESUS & MARY walk down aisle. JOHN the APOSTLE joins MARY MAGDALENE; Remaining cast, enter and bow. All interact with Audience as they joyfully exit Center).

NARRATOR: Ethan, the Crossmaker, was added to the list of disciples on that first Easter Morning. May we, too, take up our crosses–to go and make disciples of all nations as Jesus has taught us, to believe, and want, the Resurrection that awaits us all.

BLACKOUT   MUSICAL POSTLUDE   THE END